Basic
Media Skills
through Games

Basic
Media Skills
through Games

Irene Wood Bell
Media Specialist
Denver Public Schools

Jeanne E. Wieckert
Media Specialist
Denver Public Schools

Warren G. Wieckert
Illustrator

Libraries Unlimited, Inc. - Littleton, Colo. - 1979

LIBRARIES UNLIMITED, INC.
P.O. Box 263
Littleton, Colorado 80160

Library of Congress Cataloging in Publication Data

Bell, Irene Wood, 1944-
    Basic media skills through games.

    1. Educational games—Handbooks, manuals, etc.
2. Instructional materials centers—Handbooks, manuals,
etc. 3. Library orientation—Handbooks, manuals, etc.
I. Wieckert, Jeanne E., 1939-   joint author.
II. Title.
LB1029.G3B45   372.1'3   79-941
ISBN 0-87287-194-0

This book is dedicated to

our students: past, present and future.

Without them we would not have

developed the games and materials upon which

this book is based.

TABLE OF CONTENTS

PRIMARY—Grades 1-3

INTERMEDIATE—Grades 4-6

INTERMEDIATE—Grades 4-6

INTERMEDIATE—Grades 4-6 (cont'd)

INTERMEDIATE—Grades 4-6

INTERMEDIATE—Grades 4-6 (cont'd)

FOREWORD

Basic Media Skills through Games presents 74 games that can be used in a variety of combinations to teach the progression of skills necessary for elementary school students to effectively use the IMC (Instructional Materials Center). This progression involves introducing students to the IMC, explaining the logic and use of the card catalog, teaching the structure and application of the Dewey Decimal Classification, identifying reference books and their uses, and demonstrating the functions and applications of basic audiovisual (AV) hardware and software. Within the five sections of the book, games are presented in a sequence beginning with primary grades (introductory games) and going through the sixth grade (more advanced concepts and reinforcement of basics), in order that media specialists and teachers using the book might have a suggested structure for using the activities in the IMC. (Appendix I presents a suggested progression of IMC skills that can be utilized in elementary school programs.) Each game has been tried and refined by the authors in their respective media centers before it ever found its way onto paper, and each has been found to contribute to students' learning how to use the IMC to their best advantage (see test results reported on page 17).

The key to effectively using *Basic Media Skills through Games* is the variety of types of games and their adaptability to a wide range of situations. There are card games, dice games, board games, puzzles, hands-on games, location games, and identification games. All of them make use of inexpensive materials readily available in most schools; and once a game is set up, it can be used repeatedly, thereby further decreasing expense. Variations of games are suggested in many cases, expanding their applicability. Some games involve team efforts, while others call for individual responses; furthermore, many can be used as either a team or an individual exercise, depending upon the needs of any given group. The elements of competition and cooperation have been found to be very effective in transmitting and reinforcing skills, and for this reason, games are structured so that winners (teams or individuals) can emerge, which always adds an air of interest for students. (Media specialists can decide whether or not actual prizes will be awarded, and some may wish to use points to help determine grades.) Some games require checking on results by the media specialist, while others are self-checking or have students check on one another (with the media specialist available as arbiter). In all, the potential uses of the games to teach and reinforce skills depend solely upon the needs and imagination of the media specialist. It should also be noted that some transfer of IMC-related concepts to classroom situations will take place, although the games in this volume are not especially classroom-oriented. (A second volume by the authors will present more specifically classroom-structured activities.)

Among the special features of *Basic Media Skills through Games* is the section on the types and uses of AV hardware and software. Other sources of games may include a smattering of such activities or ones that can be adapted to AV use, but this book presents a series of specifically AV-related games. They range from teaching students to recognize basic equipment and know the uses of it to teaching them how to operate the individual pieces. Thus, activities are practical and not totally theoretical, which allows students to gain a firm grasp of the uses of AV.

The lists of materials and instructions for each game are essentially complete and self-contained, although a few games will refer back to a prototype presented before that contains long lists of questions, book titles, author names, etc., that can be used as samples for more than one game. Such references are clearly noted in the listing of materials for any games of this nature. Beyond that and the general principles of variety and adaptability, a few seemingly mundane guidelines must be set. Noting these points prior to setting up the games for actual play will, however, possibly prevent confusion, inconvenience, or destruction of materials. First, the game to be used should be read thoroughly by the media specialist far enough in advance to make the materials, as some will require a few hours to prepare. Also, keeping the book handy during play will help if consultation of the rules in some of the more complex games is required. Paper materials (whether of posterboard, oak-tag board, index cards, etc.) can and should be laminated in advance of play to ensure their survival if multiple use is desired (clear contact paper or "Seal Laminating Film" will suffice). Gameboards can be copied directly from the book, the easiest method being to place the illustration of the gameboard under an opaque projector to display the board on a piece of posterboard taped to a wall; then simply trace over the projected image. The choice of eraseable (Vis-a-Vis®) pens was made to facilitate multiple use of materials; non-eraseable (Sharpie®) pens are suggested when materials are to be of a permanent nature. (Any pens of similar qualities can be used, of course.) The games lend themselves to any number of adaptations and variations. In many cases, the level of difficulty can be altered by substituting different questions or lists. Card games and puzzles dealing with authors and book titles can be adapted to a particular group's interests by substituting their selections of favorite books or an endless variety of other lists. Each IMC will suggest adaptations to its own students, materials, and operations, and the authors encourage media specialists to make the games relevant to students' immediate situations.

Once the materials are assembled, establishing basic procedures within the classroom can help to eliminate potential problems. Most important, the media specialist should explain the game to students thoroughly at the outset and make sure that all students understand the rules before proceeding. When teams are called for, instructions often require that a team leader be chosen; the method for doing so is often left to the discretion of the media specialist, as some will prefer to appoint leaders while others may prefer that students select from among themselves (by any number of processes). Similarly, media specialists may wish to alter the suggested methods of determining order of play; the authors frequently suggest alphabetical order by last name, but any method that demonstrates impartiality (e.g., drawing lots) would be acceptable. As for direction of play around a circle, going to the left or right is optional, naturally, so long as it is done consistently and does not confuse students or interfere with play. Finally, instructions include directions that students replace materials in the containers provided, but the media specialist will want to review any previously used game's materials prior to replay in order to be sure that all parts are present and in good enough repair to use.

An IMC is an exciting place, not only to media specialists but to any students who will seek out information on their special interests, for there is something for each student in an IMC. The main objective of a media specialist is to aid each student in satisfying his or her needs and interests in the IMC. While satisfying these needs and interests, the media specialist can share the excitement of media with students by conveying a supportive attitude, providing them orientation to the IMC, and imparting some basic "library" skills. These basic skills can be acquired through various modes of learning; however, students prefer learning such basic skills through playing educational games and they also retain information acquired in this manner. *Basic Media Skills through Games* will allow the media specialist to structure a program of such games that will present students with the opportunity to both learn and have fun. Enjoy!

I.W.B.
J.E.W.

A Note about Test Results

As noted above, actual use of these games has been made in the schools in which the authors work. When their students were given the McGraw-Hill "Comprehensive Test of Basic Skills" (BTBS®), Level II, Form S, results over a two-year period were dramatic. After spending only 25 minutes per week working on skills activities, students often scored considerably higher in reference skills than in reading skills. The following are sample scores for the same group of pupils over a two-year period:

FALL 1977 (5th grade)		FALL 1978 (6th grade)	
Total Reading	Reference Skills	Total Reading	Reference Skills
4.6	5.5	5.5	11.7
1.7	2.2	1.8	4.0
4.8	5.5	5.5	10.4
6.2	8.6	8.5	11.7

* * *

ACKNOWLEDGMENTS

We are most appreciative of the help and criticism given us by the following people:

Ms. Lucile Hatch, Professor Emeritus, Graduate School of Librarianship, University of Denver; Denver, Colorado

Mr. Dennis E. Winters, English Coordinator, Ipswich Junior High School; Ipswich, Massachusetts

Dr. Norma Livo, Professor of Education, University of Colorado at Denver; Denver, Colorado

PART I

BREAKING THE ICE:
Introduction to the Instructional Materials Center

An introduction to the IMC that includes the active participation of students, competition, and fun will motivate students to quickly learn the arrangement of the IMC, basic IMC vocabulary, and the parts of a book. Some alphabetizing games are included in this chapter since alphabetizing is a basic skill that is necessary for working in the IMC.

Audio visual materials that may be helpful in introducing the IMC are:

1) "Books Talk Back" (Library Filmstrip Center; sound filmstrip; 9 minutes; color).

2) "Exploring Library Land" (*Adventures in Library Land*; Educational Enrichment Materials; sound filmstrip; 8 minutes; color).

3) "Meet Mr. Library Manners" (*Adventures in Library Land*; Educational Enrichment Materials; sound filmstrip; 8 minutes; color).

4) "Exploring the Library" (*Using the Elementary School Library*; SVE; sound filmstrip; 15 minutes; color).

5) "Getting to Know Books" (*Using the Elementary School Library*; SVE; sound filmstrip; 15 minutes; color).

6) "The Parts of a Book" (*Using the Library Effectively*; Creative Visuals; transparencies; color).

7) "The Parts of a Book" (*Library Services*; Eye Gate House; filmstrip; color).

8) "Getting Acquainted with the Parts of a Book" (*How to Use the Library*; Educational Progress Corporation; audio cassettes; Tapes 4 and 5; 20 minutes each tape).

PURPOSE: To help primary students learn about the physical structure of the IMC, how to care for books, and certain aspects of books.

GRADE LEVEL: Primary—1st and 2nd grades

TIME: 25 minutes

NUMBER: Best played with a maximum of 16 students

METHOD OF CHECKING: Media specialist

MATERIALS:
1) 1 timer
2) 30 3x4" colored poster board cards with questions on the front and the answers on the back, such as:

> Where is the circulation desk (or area) located?
>
> Where is the area (or table) for returning books?
>
> What would happen if a returning book is left on a table or placed back on the shelf? (it would be a "lost" book, for the media specialist would still have the sign-out card and the student is still held responsible for the book)
>
> Where are periodicals or magazines located?
>
> On what shelves are the easy books found?
>
> Why should books be used only when hands are clean?
>
> When turning the pages of a book, why should they be turned at the fore edges? (so as not to tear the pages)
>
> Why is a book opened no further than the flat surface of a table? (so the back will not break)
>
> How does one mark the place in a book when reading must stop?
>
> What might happen if a pencil is used as a bookmark? (the book might become marked)
>
> What might happen if pages are turned from the edges near the bound side? (they might tear)
>
> What happens when an open book is turned face down? (the spine could be damaged)

What happens when a page corner is creased to mark the place? (it becomes dog-eared and eventually tears loose)

Why shouldn't crayons be used around most books? (they could be used to mark-up a book, causing words or pictures to be lost)

What should you do if a page gets torn at home? (bring it to the media specialist to mend with special tape)

Why shouldn't ordinary Scotch tape be used to mend pages? (it turns yellow with age and dirt collects around its edges)

When checking out a book, what information should be written on the sign-out card? (name and room number)

How long can a book be kept out of the IMC before it is overdue?

Why is the capital letter E on picture books important? (it designates a book as "easy")

What is an author? (the person who writes a book, story, poem, etc.)

What is a title? (the name of a book, story, poem, etc.)

What does an illustrator do to a book? (draws the pictures)

Why is the letter under the E, on a book spine, important? (it is the letter with which the author's last name begins)

What is the "spine" of a book? (the place where all the pages come together and are held in place—the backbone)

How are books arranged on the shelves? (in alphabetical order according to the author's last name)

Where are signed book cards placed?

Where are pencils and colored paper bookmarks kept?

Where is the pencil sharpener located?

What are fiction books? (created or made-up stories)

What does non-fiction mean? (books that are based on fact)

3) Large manila envelope (9x12") for materials.

PROCEDURE:

1) Decide which questions can be used successfully with first graders and which should be reserved for second graders.

2) Prior to using the question cards, thoroughly discuss everything that they cover with the students.

3) Divide the students into two evenly matched teams and choose a leader for each.

(Procedures list continues on page 24)

4) Each team sits in a semi-circle on the floor, or use chairs, with the leader in the middle.

5) The team leaders are to guess a number between 1 and 10. The number that matches or is closest to the number that the media specialist has written down designates which team goes first.

6) The media specialist asks any question of the first team and sets the timer for one minute.

7) Team members are to confer with each other and the leader is to pick someone to answer before the timer rings.

8) If the answer is correct, the team receives two points; if not, the opposing team has a chance to correctly answer and then take an additional turn.

9) The team with the most points wins.

10) Game may be played one or more times, depending upon class interest and the need to reinforce IMC basics.

■ ■ ■

<<<>>><<<>>><<<>>><<<>>><<<>>><<<>>><<<>>><<<>>><<<>>><<<>>>

CLIMB THE MOUNTAIN

<<<>>><<<>>><<<>>><<<>>><<<>>><<<>>><<<>>><<<>>><<<>>><<<>>>

PURPOSE: To gain practice in using IMC vocabulary and to demonstrate proper IMC procedures.

GRADE LEVEL: Primary—1st and 2nd grades

TIME: 25 minutes

NUMBER: Best played with a maximum of 16 students

METHOD OF CHECKING: Media specialist

MATERIALS:
1) Flannel board, on which to place items (2) and (3) below.

2) Felt mountain with seven places on each side to which a felt mountain climber can be affixed (size can vary).

3) Two felt mountain climbers.

(Materials list continues on page 26)

4)   One die.

5)   20 3x4" cards with instructions or questions on them, such as:

> Choose a book from the shelf and show how to turn the pages correctly.
>
> What is the name of a book called? (title)
>
> Go to the listening center and show how to get ready to listen to a story.
>
> Show how to put a book back on the shelf.
>
> Show where the magazines are found in the IMC.
>
> Who does the art work in a book? (illustrator)

6)   Large manila envelope (12x15") for materials.

PROCEDURE:

1)   Divide the group into two teams.

2)   The teams form two lines and sit facing the flannel board.

3)   The first person on each team rolls the die to determine the team that starts. Thereafter, the teams alternate turns.

4)   The media specialist draws a card and reads the instruction or the question.

5)   If the player follows the instruction or answers the question correctly, the felt mountain climber representing that person's team can be moved one place up the mountain.

6)   If incorrect, the other team gets a chance to move up the mountain by answering or following the instruction correctly.

7)   If neither team is correct, the media specialist gives the correct answer or follows the instruction correctly and neither mountain climber moves up the mountain.

8)   The first team to move its mountain climber to the top of the mountain wins.

■ ■ ■

PURPOSE: To gain practice in becoming familiar with IMC terminology.

GRADE LEVEL: 3rd and 4th grades

TIME: 30-35 minutes

NUMBER: Best played with a maximum of 16 students

METHOD OF CHECKING: Media specialist

MATERIALS:
1)   16 cards of oak-tag board (9x12") in the shape of monsters; 4 "Monster Match" cards of the same color make a set—for a total of 4 sets.

2)   160 2x2" colored posterboard cards—10 cards to a set, for 16 sets— with an IMC term printed on each. For the first set, use the first 10 terms in the list; start the second list with the eleventh term, continue to the bottom, and return to the top of the list to finish that set; and so on to complete 16 sets. Do this for both 3rd and 4th grades.

3rd grade	**4th grade**
author	same as 3rd grade plus:
title	
fiction books	index
table of contents	publishing company
card catalog	appendix
illustrator	collective biography
easy fiction	individual biography
Caldecott Medal Award Winners	Newbery Medal Award Winners
title card	atlases, maps, globes
author card	foreword
subject card	encyclopedia
call number	title page
page numbers	spine of book
body of book	glossary
dictionary	guide cards in card catalog
copyright date	bibliography
	preface

(Materials list continues on page 28)

3) 160 6x3" oak-tag strips with definitions corresponding to the terms on the vocabulary cards printed on each strip—10 strips to a set for a total of 16 sets. On the back of the strips, indicate grade level and number of set (1-16). Do this for both 3rd and 4th grades. (See "Go Fish," page 52, for definitions.)

4) Master sheet of definitions, corresponding to the terms on the vocabulary cards; dry-mounted to a piece of colored posterboard.

5) 32 6x9" envelopes for vocabulary cards. On the bottom of each envelope, indicate grade level and number of set (1-16).

6) Two 6x9" envelopes for the definition strips; one for each grade.

7) An appropriately sized cardboard box or a large manila envelope (16x20") for storing envelopes and "Monster Match" cards.

PROCEDURE:

1) Students count off in fours and divide into groups, one each around a set of tables.

2) Each player is given a "Monster Match" card and an envelope of vocabulary cards.

3) Each player first must alphabetize the vocabulary cards and place them on the "Monster Match" card.

4) The media specialist then places the oak-tag definition strips (of the same set numbers as the vocabulary card sets) face down in the center of each table.

5) Players take turns picking a definition strip and reading the definition and set number.

6) The player who has the vocabulary card (with corresponding set number) on his or her "Monster Match" card that matches the definition calls out "Match." That player takes the strip and places it on the "Monster Match" card next to the vocabulary card.

7) The player who matched the definition with the vocabulary card then reads the next definition.

8) Play continues in this manner until one player has completed a "Monster Match" card.

9) When a player is finished and raises a hand to indicate so, the media specialist should check the card.

10) If correct, the player scores 7 points, places the vocabulary cards back in the envelope, piles the definition strips neatly, and can choose a center activity.

11) If incorrect, the media specialist takes off any incorrect definitions and places them back in the center pile.

12) In either case, play is resumed until everyone has completed a "Monster Match" card.

13) Point totals can be as follows for multiple rounds of "Monster Match":

first round	7 points
second round	6 points
third round	5 points
fourth round	4 points

■ ■ ■

BEGINNING, MIDDLE, OR END

PURPOSE: To give primary students practice in learning the alphabet and dividing it into beginning, middle, or end.

GRADE LEVEL: Primary—1st and 2nd grades

TIME: Form A—25 minutes
            Form B—25 minutes

NUMBER: Best played with a maximum of 16 students

METHOD OF CHECKING: Media specialist

MATERIALS:
1) 3 8x10" colored posterboards with the words "beginning," "middle," or "end" clearly printed (one word to a board), to be used as the playing board.

2) 3 8x10" colored posterboards, one for each section of the alphabet (A-G, H-P, Q-Z), and each with the corresponding letters of the alphabet printed clearly.

3) 52 3x3" colored posterboard cards with a letter of the alphabet printed clearly on each card; a total of two sets each with a complete alphabet.

4) Large manila envelope (12x15") for the materials.

PROCEDURE: First divide the students into two teams even in number.

Form A
1) Display the full alphabet in the three sections—A-G, H-P, Q-Z—on charts or write it on a chalkboard.

2) A student is chosen to come up in front of the group and randomly select a letter from the prepared cards.

3) When the letter is chosen, the student calls upon a student from the opposing team to place that letter on the playing board in the proper category—beginning, middle, or end—of the alphabet.

4) If the letter is placed correctly, the first student returns to the group, the second student stays at the front, selects a new letter and calls upon another student to place it.

5) If the student places the letter incorrectly, he sits down and another student is chosen to place the letter.

6) Give points for each correct answer; or award a happy smile badge to the student answering correctly the most times.

7) The game continues in this fashion until all the cards are used up or until the specialist determines that the alphabet charts can be removed from display.

Form B

1) Same as above, with the exception that the alphabet is not on display.

2) The students play the game by memory.

■ ■ ■

HOT OR COLD

PURPOSE: To help primary students learn to shelve easy books properly.

GRADE LEVEL: Primary—1st and 2nd grades

TIME: 25 minutes

NUMBER: Best played with a maximum of 10 students

METHOD OF CHECKING: Media specialist

MATERIALS:
1) A variety of 20-25 easy books.

PROCEDURE:
1) Before the students arrive, place in a pile the books chosen from the easy shelves.

2) Have the students sit in a semi-circle in front of the media specialist.

3) Hold up a book, read the whole call number:

E	or	E	or	E
M		Miller,		Mil
		Edna		

(depending on how the books are labeled).

4) Ask if the author's initial is at the beginning, middle, or end of the alphabet. This procedure gives a clue as to where to start.

5) Choose the player who has correctly answered to go to the shelf, find the correct shelf, and shelve the book.

6) As that player gets closer to the shelf, say: "you're getting warmer, you're getting hot, you're ready to burst into flames," and so on.

   As a player moves away from the correct shelf, say: "you're cooling off, you're cold, you're frozen solid," and so on.

7) When a player has correctly identified the shelf, she or he is to place the book correctly on the shelf.

VARIATION: As players learn where books should go on the shelves, choose a player to say "hot," "cold," and so on.

■ ■ ■

SORTING OUT

PURPOSE: To practice alphabetizing authors' names—both one-letter alphabetizing and two-letter alphabetizing.

GRADE LEVEL: 3rd grade through 5th grade

TIME: Form A—50 minutes
          Form B—50 minutes

NUMBER: Best played with a maximum of 16 students

METHOD OF CHECKING: Media specialist

MATERIALS:
1)   Two dice.

2)   1 to 16 egg cartons—one for each player.

3)   A minimum of 50 "extra" author cards will be needed prior to beginning play, and to that should be added,

4)   5 author cards per player (whether for one- or two-letter alphabetizing). Thus, for 16 players, a total of 130 cards would be needed (50 base and 80 added, 5 per player). Author names can be taken from the following lists, depending upon purpose, but more in each letter would be needed to prepare 130 cards:

      a) Author cards for one-letter alphabetizing, such as:

Aardema	Warner	McGovern	Johnston
Alexander	Peck	Miller	Juster
Alcott	Lionni	Nesbit	Keene
Arthur	MacGregor	Norton	Kipling
Aylesworth	Farley	Nourse	Parish
Eberle	Fisher	O'Dell	Politi
Elting	Bond	Olney	Quackerbush
Epstein	Brink	Orton	Quinn
Fatio	Bulla	Damato	Radlauer
Schulz	Carey	Duprey	Rey
Travers	Cleary	Ingrams	Rockwell
Tolkien	Colby	Ipcar	Sasek
Untermeyer	Dixon	Jacobs	Kettelkamp

(List of author names continues on page 34)

Lawson	Sleator
L'Engle	Taylor
Gag	Uchida
George	Wahl
Goetz	Weiss
Hawes	Yolen
Henry	Yates
Hoke	

b) Author cards for two-letter alphabetizing, such as:

Adler	Erdoes	Lofting	Rich
Agle	Farber	Luce	Roberts
Aiken	Fenner	Mackay	Rumsey
Arden	Fife	McCall	Sawyer
Atwood	Flora	Mendoza	Scheele
Babbitt	Foster	Miers	Selsam
Belting	Galdone	Moody	Sharmat
Bishop	Geis	Naden	Snyder
Boehn	Gidal	Newsome	Terris
Branley	Godden	Nitsche	Thiele
Calhoun	Graves	Norris	Tobias
Cerf	Haas	Nyce	Tresselt
Chandler	Heide	Oakley	Tunis
Clymer	Hillert	O'Brien	Waber
Cohen	Hofsinde	Olds	Weber
Dahl	Hurd	Orgel	Whitney
De Jong	Kahl	Otto	Wilder
Dobrin	Keats	Parker	Woolley
Drury	Kirk	Peet	Zaffo
Dunn	Kjelgaard	Pine	Zemach
Eager	Knight	Poe	Zim
Eckert	Lauber	Pringle	Zolotow
Edmonds	Leckie	Radlauer	
Emberley	Lipkind	Renick	

5) Large manila envelope (12x15") for the materials.

PROCEDURE:

Form A [single-letter alphabetizing] :
1) Each student is to sit where an inverted egg carton has been placed (at grouped tables or on the floor, students in a circle).

2) The media specialist deals out five cards to each player and places the remainder of the deck in the center of the group.

3) Players are to place the cards in the slots of the inverted egg carton in the order dealt, beginning with the first slot through the fifth slot. (The object will be to alphabetize five cards (A-Z) by first letter of author's name, gaining the cards to do so by drawing and discarding until a sequence of five different letters is in order).

4) Each player throws the dice to see who obtains the highest number; player with the highest number goes first. (Play goes to the right around the circle until the original player starts again.)

5) The first card dealt to each player always remains in the first slot of that person's carton, and becomes the starting point from which a player begins to alphabetize.

6) Each player takes a turn drawing from the deck or discard pile (always discarding as part of the turn) until one player has five author cards in first-letter alphabetical order, beginning with the lowest to the highest letter (A-Z direction). (For instance, a player with A-B-C would discard another A, B, or C in hopes of a D or E card.)

7) The player who correctly alphabetizes all five different-letter author cards first wins the game and scores five points. The remaining players score one point for each author correctly alphabetized.

Form B [two-letter alphabetizing] :
1) Steps one through four are the same as Form A, but the object is alphabetizing author cards *within one letter*.

2) Before the first round begins, players decide which letter each is going to collect. (Example: A—Adler, Agle, Aiken, Arden, Atwood.)

3) During the first round, players may only choose a card from the pile face down or the top card of the discard pile. If they pick a card they can use, they are to place it in a slot and discard another card. (They *cannot* alphabetize during the first round.)

4) In round two and each succeeding round, players may:
   a) choose a card from the deck face down, or
   b) choose any card from the discard pile, or
   c) ask anyone in the circle for a card beginning with the letter they are collecting, provided that they have a card that the other player can use (in other words, trade useful cards), or
   d) move two cards around in their carton so that author cards are in order by the second letter.

5) The player who correctly alphabetizes the author cards first for one letter wins the game and scores seven points. The remaining players score one point for each author card correctly alphabetized.

■　■　■

PURPOSE: To gain familiarity with the arrangement of the IMC and the location of materials.

GRADE LEVEL: 3rd grade through 6th grade

TIME: 25 minutes

NUMBER: Best played with a maximum of 16 students

METHOD OF CHECKING: Media specialist

MATERIALS:
1) 16 9x12" oak-tag "Encounter" cards with a diagram of the IMC drawn on them. Slits are made adjacent to the items or areas that are to be labeled.

2) Paper clips are inserted into the slits.

   [Illustration of "Encounter" game appears on page 37.]

3) 16 sets of oak-tag board labels, ½x3", the cards in each set corresponding in number to the IMC parts to be identified on the "Encounter" card. Some suggested labels are:

   card catalog
   reference center
   check-out desk

4) Transparency or diagram of the IMC, to be discussed with students before beginning the game.

5) Large manila envelope (12x15") for the materials.

PROCEDURE:
1) Divide group into two teams.

2) Each student is given an "Encounter" card and an envelope with labels.

3) The media specialist recalls the transparency/diagram shown previously, when the arrangement of the IMC was discussed.

(Procedures continue on page 38)

ENCOUNTER

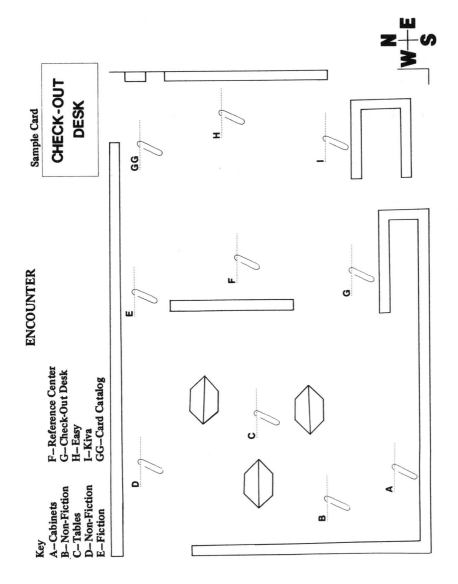

Key
A–Cabinets
B–Non-Fiction
C–Tables
D–Non-Fiction
E–Fiction

F–Reference Center
G–Check-Out Desk
H–Easy
I–Kiva
GG–Card Catalog

Sample Card

CHECK-OUT
DESK

4) Each student is to label each part of the diagram on the "Encounter" card by placing the proper label under the paper clip adjacent to that part of the IMC.

5) Each player raises a hand when finished and the media specialist checks the "Encounter" cards. If correct, the player than chooses a book to read.

6) The team that places all of its cards on the "Encounter" board first wins.

■ ■ ■

PURPOSE: To reinforce knowledge of the terms used to describe parts of a book and IMC terminology (previously discussed with students).

GRADE LEVEL: Intermediate—4th grade

TIME: 50 minutes

NUMBER: Best played with a maximum of 16 students

METHOD OF CHECKING: Media specialist

MATERIALS:
1) Master sheet of words and their definitions, corresponding to the book terms and IMC terms previously discussed with students; dry-mounted to a piece of colored posterboard. "Fill-in-the-blanks" sentences should be made for each term. The following book terms and suggested sentences are suitable for the 4th grade:

call number	foreword
title	publishing company
author	glossary
title page	index
illustrator	appendix
page number	bibliography
table of contents	copyright date
body of book	

The "teapot" is a small dictionary usually found at the end of a book. (glossary)

The "teapot" is a number that identifies the book by subject and author. (call number)

The "teapot" is found on the upper left-hand corner of a catalog card. (call number)

This "teapot" is the name of a book, play, poem, etc. (title)

You can find a book by its "teapot." (title)

This "teapot" is a talented person who writes books, poems, stories, or articles. (author)

(Suggested sentences continue on page 40)

A "teapot" that is found at the beginning of the book that contains five important pieces of information. (title page)

This "teapot" is a talented person who draws pictures for books. (illustrator)

This "teapot" is most helpful in locating chapters or stories and their page numbers. (table of contents)

This "teapot" is the material in a book that is to be read or studied. (body of book)

It is not unusual to find these "teapots" in the table of contents. (page numbers)

It is not unusual to find these "teapots" in the table of contents. (chapters, story titles)

Information may be found above or below these "teapots" on a page. (page numbers)

This "teapot" is a brief synopsis of the book found at the beginning of it. (foreword)

This "teapot" publishes the book. (publishing company)

This "teapot" is an alphabetically arranged list of what is in a book, telling on what pages to find various topics. (index)

This "teapot" offers additional material at the end of a book. (appendix)

This "teapot" is a list of books or magazine articles on a particular subject and is found at the end of a work. (bibliography)

This "teapot" is the year in which the book was published. (copyright date)

This "teapot" is very important to an author after the book is published, so that another person cannot copy or reuse the material without permission from the author or publisher. (copyright)

These "teapots," located throughout a book, are additional materials to help a person understand the written word. They are drawn by a "teapot." (illustrations, illustrator)

2) Chalkboard and chalk.

3) Large manila envelope (9x12") for the master sheet.

PROCEDURE:

1) Divide a chalkboard into three sections, with the headings "beginning," "middle," and "end." Under each heading, write the terms that have been previously discussed.

2) One player (the "contestant") leaves the IMC.

3) Media specialist picks out one term, and each remaining player thinks of a sentence with that term that will adequately identify it. Substitute the word "teapot" for the term.

4) Contestant comes back into the IMC.

5) Media specialist calls on students to recite their sentences to the contestant, replacing the selected term with the word "teapot." The contestant then guesses the term to be used.

6) If the term is correctly guessed, the contestant is allowed to go out of the IMC again. (Suggest no more than two times per contestant.)

7) If the term is not correctly guessed, the contestant sits down and is replaced by the player who thought of the best sentence—to be determined by the media specialist.

8) For each term correctly identified and for the best sentence given in each round, players score one point.

ALTERNATIVE PROCEDURE:

1) If the make-up of the class warrants it, a dittoed list of terms and their definitions may be prepared for each player.

or

2) Players sit in a circle and the media specialist gives the sentences, and the players guess the "teapot."

■ ■ ■

ARE YOU FAMILIAR WITH???

PURPOSE: To review the parts of a book and to develop speed in deciding their location.

GRADE LEVEL: Intermediate—5th and 6th grades

TIME: 50 minutes

NUMBER: Best played with a maximum of 16 students

METHOD OF CHECKING: Self-checking

MATERIALS:
1) Two gameboards, each made from 22x28" colored posterboards. Divide into 3 unequal sections and label, as shown below:

ARE YOU FAMILIAR WITH???	
BEGINNING - 1	MIDDLE - 2
	END - 3

(Parts of a book)

2) 82 3x4" colored posterboard player cards—41 cards per set for 2 sets. Number the backs of each set of cards from 1 to 41. On the front of each card, letter one of the parts of a book from the following list:

Beginning	Middle	End
dedication	chapters	glossary
preface	poems	index of authors
title page	plays	footnotes
author	orations	index
editor	articles	epilogue
prologue	footnotes	appendix
frontispiece	essays	index of titles
acknowledgments	narrative poems	author synopsis
edition	stories	index of first lines
title	chapter bibliography	bibliography for the
illustrator	story illustrations	entire book
translator	chapter questions	
foreword	chapter headings	
copyright date		
table of contents		
place of printing		
list of illustrations		
index abbreviations		

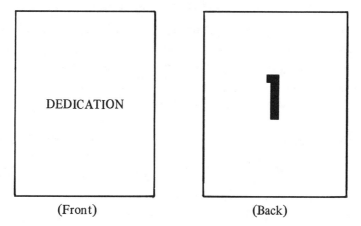

(Front)   (Back)

3) 82 3x3" colored posterboard team cards (41 cards per set) for the team leader to use. They should have the same numbers and terms on them as are printed on the other sets. This time, however, the number is on the front and the answer is on the back with its proper number (corresponding to beginning-1; middle-2; end-3) in the lower right-hand corner [see illustration on page 44].

(Materials list continues on page 44)

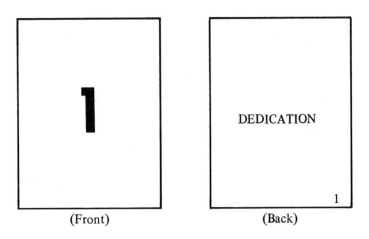

(Front)   (Back)

4)   Large manila envelope (9x12") for the materials.

PROCEDURE:

1)   Divide the students into two evenly matched teams, and choose team leaders.

2)   The gameboards are placed in front of the teams, one to a team.

3)   The media specialist distributes the player cards to the players.

4)   Each team leader picks one of the team cards and holds it up with the number facing the players (the answer toward himself).

5)   The player holding that number takes his or her player card, goes to the gameboard, and places the card on the appropriate section (1, 2, or 3), term side facing up.

6)   If correct, it stays there. If incorrect, the team leader takes the card and uses it for review at the end of the game.

7)   Play continues with the leader displaying team cards to be matched by player cards until all cards are used.

8)   For each card placed correctly, a player scores one point.

■ ■ ■

BOOK BINGO

PURPOSE: To demonstrate the ability to identify the uses of various parts of a book.

GRADE LEVEL: Intermediate—5th and 6th grades

TIME: 15 minutes per round

NUMBER: Best played with a maximum of 16 students

METHOD OF CHECKING: Media specialist

MATERIALS:
1) 20 6x6½" colored posterboard cards, each containing book terms (see "Go Fish," page 52, for a list of terms and definitions):

B	**O**[1]	**O**[2]	**K**
Index	Title	Editor	Table of Contents
Author	Bibliography	Copyright Date	Illustrator
Acknowl-edgment	Edition	Title Page	Prologue
Glossary	Appendix	Dedication	Foreword

(Materials list continues on page 46)

2) Plastic tokens—20 each in a small envelope or cloth pouch—for each player.

3) Letter-size envelopes or cloth pouches, one per player.

4) Master sheet of book terms and the definitions corresponding to those terms, which should be previously discussed with students; dry-mounted to a piece of colored posterboard (again, see "Go Fish," page 52, for a list of definitions).

5) Large manila envelope (16x20") for the materials.

PROCEDURE:

1) Distribute the "Book Bingo" cards and plastic tokens to each player.

2) Media specialist is to give a definition or show a particular part of a book and mark the answer with a check mark (✓) on the master sheet.

3) Players cover the appropriate space on their "Book Bingo" cards as they find the answers.

4) As soon as a player has covered four spaces in a row in any direction, that person should indicate "Book Bingo" by raising a hand.

5) The media specialist then checks that player's card, verifying the win.

6) Players clear their cards, exchange them with neighbors, and start over again. Four cards apiece is a good number for review.

7) The winning player in each instance is to receive a certain number of points—to be determined in advance by the media specialist.

■ ■ ■

◇◇◇◇◇◇◇◇◇◇◇◇◇◇◇◇◇◇◇◇◇◇◇◇◇◇◇◇◇◇◇◇◇◇◇◇◇◇◇

USE YOUR BOOK

◇◇◇◇◇◇◇◇◇◇◇◇◇◇◇◇◇◇◇◇◇◇◇◇◇◇◇◇◇◇◇◇◇◇◇◇◇◇◇

PURPOSE: To gain practice using the table of contents and index in a book.

GRADE LEVEL: Intermediate—5th and 6th grades

TIME: 25 minutes

NUMBER: Best played with a maximum of 16 students

METHOD OF CHECKING: Media specialist

MATERIALS:
1)   16 copies of an English textbook—any textbook may be used with questions appropriate to its own table of contents and index.

2)   Blackboard.

3)   List of appropriate questions, designed to show whether the index or table of contents (or both) provided the answers, and what those answers are. [The following questions were developed for use with *Exploring the English Experience in Language* (by Hand, Harsh, Ney, and Shange; Laidlaw Brothers, 1977)] :

On what page would *the two parts of a sentence* be found? (table of contents—p. 104)

Is there anything in this book about *giving instructions*? (table of contents—p. 146)

Is there anything in this book about *recipes*? (index—pp. 148-49)

Can anything be found about the *Russian alphabet* (Cyrillic alphabet) in this book? (index—pp. 126-27)

Is there anything about *telling jokes*? (index—pp. 112-13; table of contents—p. 112)

Is there anything about *unusual words*? (index—pp. 12-13; table of contents—p. 12)

On what page is there information about *special codes*? (table of contents p. 156; index—pp. 156-57)

Is *Steve Allen* mentioned in this book? (index—p. 178)

PROCEDURE:

1) The group is divided into two evenly matched teams, and a team leader is appointed.

2) The media specialist writes, for example, "the two parts of a sentence" on the blackboard.

3) The two teams attempt to find the entry in the table of contents or the index.

4) The student who locates the entry should raise a hand.

5) The media specialist calls on the student to answer.

6) If the student answers correctly, a point is scored for that team.

7) If the student is incorrect, the other team has a chance to answer correctly and score a point.

8) The media specialist continues writing the underlined portion of the questions on the blackboard and continues play in the above manner.

9) The team with the most points wins.

■ ■ ■

FIND THAT WORD

PURPOSE: To gain practice in becoming familiar with IMC terminology.

GRADE LEVEL: Intermediate—5th and 6th grades

TIME: 50 minutes

NUMBER: Best played with a maximum of 16 students

METHOD OF CHECKING: Media specialist

MATERIALS:
1) 16 Vis-a-Vis® pens.

2) 16 9x12" well-laminated tagboard "Find That Word" cards with ten definitions printed on each card; answers supplied in this illustration would, of course, not appear on the cards.

(List of materials continues on page 51)

FIND THAT WORD

Letter=Points

A=1
B=2
C=3
D=4
E=5
F=6
G=7
H=8
I=9
J=10
K=11
L=12
M=13
N=14
O=15
P=16

1. The c - - d c - - - - - - is where information can be found to locate a book on the shelf. (card catalog)

    Score: _____

2. A dictionary is a r - fe - - - - e b - - k. (reference book)

    Score: _____

3. A true book is called a - o - f - - - - o - book. (non-fiction)

    Score: _____

4. The numbers and letters on the spines of books that help to locate a book are the c - - l - - m - - r - . (call numbers)

    Score: _____

(Illustration continues on page 50)

Find That Word (cont'd)

Letter=Points

Q=17
R=18
S=19
T=20
U=21
V=22
W=23
X=24
Y=25
Z=26

5. F--t--- books are those whose contents are imagined or created stories. (fiction)

    Score: _____

6. The t-b-- o- c--t---- is found in the beginning of the book and gives chapters and page numbers. (table of contents)

    Score: _____

7. A-lo----- is a short dictionary found at the end of a book. (glossary)

    Score: _____

8. The t-t-- p--- of a book contains all of the important information about a book. (title page)

    Score: _____

9. The name of a book is its -i---. (title)

    Score: _____

10. An -u--o- is the person who wrote the book. (author)

    Score: _____

11. The ill------o- is the person who does the art work in a book. (illustrator)

    Score: _____

12. The -n--x is an alphabetical listing of the material in a book. (index)

    Score: _____

13. A b-og----y is a book about a person's life written by another person. (biography)

    Score: _____

14. An a--a- is a book of maps. (atlas)

    Score: _____

15. An -l-a-a- is a book that gives up-to-date general information. (almanac)

    Score: _____

(These may be given in a different order, but students need to be sure of spelling.)

3) Paper towels to wipe off the marker from "Find That Word" cards when the game is finished.

4) Large manila envelope (12x15") for the materials.

PROCEDURE:

1) Players are given a "Find That Word" card and a Vis-a-Vis® pen.

2) Players are to fill in the missing letters to complete the definitions.

3) After completing the definitions, the players compute their scores for each word by adding up the number given for each letter of the alphabet filled in to make the word. For example, title: t=20, i=9, t=20, e=5; score: 56 [the letters already supplied do not count in scoring].

4) The player with the highest score at the end of the game is the winner. All points count toward individual scores.

■ ■ ■

GO FISH

PURPOSE: To gain skill in using IMC vocabulary.

GRADE LEVEL: 3rd grade through 6th grade

TIME: 25 minutes—3rd grade
          35 minutes—4th grade
          50 minutes—5th and 6th grades

NUMBER: Best played with a maximum of 16 students

METHOD OF CHECKING: Media specialist

MATERIALS:
1a)   3rd grade—45 3x4" colored posterboard cards: a term card, a definition
      card, and a pronunciation card from a set—15 sets of term, definition,
      and pronunciation cards to a pack, for a total of 3 packs. One set of
      3 cards might look like this:

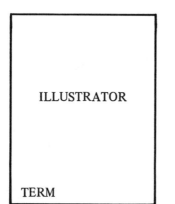

ILLUSTRATOR

TERM

An artist who makes
pictures to be used as
additional examples in
a book.

DEFINITION

(Third card in set is shown at the top of page 53)

```
┌─────────────────────────┐
│  ┌───────────────────┐  │
│  │                   │  │
│  │                   │  │
│  │                   │  │
│  │ ĭl´ə-strā´ tər    │  │
│  │                   │  │
│  │                   │  │
│  │                   │  │
│  │ PRONUNCIATION     │  │
│  └───────────────────┘  │
└─────────────────────────┘
```

Terms, definitions, and pronunciations that would be appropriate include the following:

copyright date—the year the book was published—kŏp´ē-rĭt´ dāt

author—a person who writes books, poems, stories, or articles—
    ô´thər

title—the name of a book, play, poem, etc.—tīt´l

title page—the page at the beginning of a book that contains the title,
    author's or editor's name, publisher, and place of publication—
    tīt´l pāj

illustrator—an artist who makes pictures to be used in a book—
    ĭl´ə -strā´tər

page numbers—numbers that mark pages so that material may be
    found easily—pāj nŭm´bər

table of contents—a list with page numbers of the chapters found
    within a book—tā´bəl ŭv kŏn´tĕnts

body of book—the part of a book that contains the material to be read
    or studied—bŏd´ē ŭv bŏŏk

call number—the classification number, which identifies the book by
    subject and author; a system that identifies books as "easy
    fiction" or "fiction" and their author(s)—kôl nŭm´ bər

card catalog—the index to all books in the IMC/library—kärd
    kăt´ l-ôg

dictionary—a reference in which words are entered alphabetically and
    defined—dĭk´ shə-nĕr´ ē

(List continues on page 54)

author card—a catalog card with the name of the author on the top line—ô′ thər kärd

subject card—a catalog card with the subject on the top line— sŭb′ jĭkt kärd

title card—a catalog card with the title on the top line—tĭt′l kärd

easy books—books whose contents appeal particularly to young children—ē′ zē bŏŏk

fiction books—books whose contents are imagined or created stories—fĭk′ shən bŏŏk

1b) 4th grade—the same cards as for 3rd grade, except increase the number to 17 sets (for a total of 51 cards to a pack and an overall total of 153 cards in 3 packs).

Use the same list as for 3rd grade plus:

foreword—a brief synopsis of the book found at the beginning of the book—fôr′ wərd

preface—an introduction to a book, poem, or other literary work that explains the work—prĕf′ is

appendix—additional material at the end of a book or document— ə-pĕn′ dĭks

glossary—a list of special, technical, or difficult words with explanations found within a book; a small dictionary to the book— glôs′ ə-rē

index—a list of what is in a book, telling on what pages to find topics; usually at the end of the book and arranged in alphabetical order—ĭn′ dĕks′

bibliography—a list of books on a particular subject found at the end of a work—bĭb′ lē-ŏg′ rə-fē

publishing company—a business firm that issues a book— pŭb′ lĭsh-ing kŭm′ pə-nē

encyclopedia—a book or set of books containing information on all subjects or covering major points of one subject— ĕn-sī′ klə-pē′ dē-ə

Dewey Decimal Classification System—a system of dividing non-fiction books into ten major classes by subject matter, with further subdivision in each class; named after Melvil Dewey, its inventor— dōō′ ē dĕs′ ə-məl klas′ ə-fi-kā′ shən sis′ təm

collective biography—accounts of the lives of many people gathered in one book—kə-lĕk´tiv bī-ŏg´rə-fē

individual biography—account of a person's life written by another person—ĭn´də-vĭj´ōō-əl bī-ŏg´rə-fē

atlas—any volume of tables, charts, or plates that systematically illustrates a subject—ăt´ləs

map—a representation, usually on a flat surface, of a portion of the earth or heavens—măp

globes—any body having the shape of a sphere; especially, a representation of the earth or heavenly bodies in the form of a hollow ball—glōbs

guide cards in card catalog—words or phrases on cards elevated above the level of regular cards to facilitate locating an author, title, or subject—gīd´ kärds in kärd kăt´l-ôg

1c) 5th and 6th grades—the same cards as for 3rd grade except increase the number to 20 sets (for a total of 60 cards to a pack and an overall total of 180 cards in 3 packs). Use the same list as for 3rd and 4th grades plus:

dedication—the words offering a book, poem, or the like, in honor of a friend or patron—dĕd´ə -kā´ shən

printing dates—various dates on which a work was issued—prĭnt´ĭng dāt

editor—a person who prepares an author's material for publication—ĕd´ə-tər

edition—an issue of the same newspaper or book published at different times with additions and/or changes from the original—ĭ-dĭsh´ən

index of authors—an alphabetical listing of the names of those authors who are mentioned in the book; found at the end of the book—ĭn´dĕks´ ŭv ô´thərs

prologue—an introduction to a novel, poem or other literary work, explaining the work—prō´lôg´

frontispiece—an illustration facing the title page of the book—frŭn´tĭs-pēs´

acknowledgments—an expression of thanks for any help received in writing a book, story, or article—ăk-nŏl´ĭj-mənt

translator—a person who rewrites a work from one language into another—trăns-lā´tər

(List continues on page 56)

footnotes—notes at the bottom of a page about something on that page; or a listing at the end of a book—fŏŏt´nŏt´

index of titles—an alphabetical listing of the titles of works found within the book, giving their page numbers; found at the end of the book—ĭn´dĕks´ ŭv tīt´l

epilogue—a concluding section sometimes added to a book, serving to round out or interpret the work—ĕp´ə-lôg´

author synopsis—a brief statement of the author's life, usually found at the end of a book—ô´thər sĭ-nŏp´sĭs

running title—the title of the book; it appears at the top of each page or on alternate pages—rŭn´ĭng tīt´l

place of printing—the city in which a work has been published—plās ŭv prĭnt´ĭng

list of illustrations—a listing of the pictures, diagrams, or maps found within a book—lĭst ŭv ĭl´ə-strā´shən

chapter bibliography—a list of books, articles, etc., about a particular subject; found at the end of a chapter—chăp´tər bĭb´lē-ŏg´rəfē

story illustration—a picture, diagram, or map used to explain a point or to decorate—stôr´ē ĭl´ə-strā´shən

chapter questions—a list of questions at the end of a chapter on material covered in that chapter—chăp´tər kwĕs´chəns

chapter heading—the name of the chapter; found on the upper right-hand page—chăp´tər hĕd´ĭng

index of first lines—an alphabetical listing of the first lines of poems found within an anthology, giving their page numbers; found at the end of the book—ĭn´dĕks ŭv fûrst līns

index of abbreviations—an alphabetical listing of the abbreviations found within a work, usually located at the beginning of a book—ĭn´dĕks ŭv ə-brē´vē-a´shən

Dewey Decimal Classification System—10 major classes for arranging library materials, divided according to numbers as follows:

000 General Works—reference works such as encyclopedias; works on library science, manners, and so on—jĕn´ər-əl wûrks

100 Philosophy—a basic theory, a viewpoint; the system of values by which one lives—fĭ-lŏs´ə-fe

200 Religion—the expression of man's belief in and reverence for a superhuman power recognized as the creator of the universe—ri-lij´ ən

300 Sociology—the study of human social behavior, especially the origins, organization, institutions, and development of human society—sō´sē-ŏl´ ə-jē

400 Language—any method of communicating ideas, as by a system of signs, symbols, gestures, and so on—lăng´gwĭj

500 Science—the observation, identification, description, experimental investigation, and explanation of natural phenomena—sī´əns

600 Applied Science or Technology—the application of science, especially to industrial or commercial objectives— ə-plī´ ed sī´ns ôr tĕk-nŏl´ə-jē

700 Arts and Recreation—1) the conscious production or arrangement of sounds, colors, forms, movements, or other elements in a manner to create beauty; 2) relaxation after work—ärts ănd rĕk´rē-ā´shən

800 Literature—a body of writings in prose or verse— lit´ ər-ə-chŏŏr´

900 History—a chronological record of events, as of the life or development of a people, country, or institution— his´tə-rē

cross-reference—a catalog card directing the user to another heading. The "see" reference directs one to another entry for information; the "see also" indicates additional entries—krôs ref´ ər-əns

almanac—an annual publication composed of various lists, charts, and tables of useful information in many unrelated fields—ôl´mə-năk´

Junior Book of Authors—a book of biographical and autobiographical sketches, in some detail, of modern authors of children's books— jŏŏn´yər bŏŏk ŭv ô´thər

More Junior Authors—see *Junior Book of Authors*—môr jŏŏn´yər ô´thər

vertical file—a cabinet of drawers, arranged in alphabetical order— vûr´tĭ-kəl fĭl

non-print media—any media that do not solely employ the printed word, such as slides, cassettes, transparencies, phonodiscs, sound filmstrips, etc.—nŏn-prĭnt mē´dē-ə

(List continues on page 58)

2) Master sheet of definitions for each grade, corresponding to the terms previously discussed with students; dry-mounted to a piece of colored posterboard.

3) Three large manila envelopes (12x15") for the materials.

PROCEDURE:

1) Discuss the terms to be used with the students, especially in the 3rd and 4th grades.

2) Students count off in fours and divide into four groups around each set of tables, players sitting in alphabetical order by last names.

3) The player with the initial closest to the beginning of the alphabet is the dealer.

4) Dealer shuffles the cards in a pack and distributes six cards to each player. The remaining cards are placed face down in a pile in the center of the table.

5) Dealer begins by asking any of the other players for a card to complete a set of which he holds at least one. (For example, if the dealer holds the term card in the "illustrator" set, that person may ask a player, "Do you have the definition for illustrator?") If that player holds the requested card, it must be surrendered to the player asking for it.

6) The dealer, if successful, continues to ask players for cards until a player is unable to give one. That player then says, "Go Fish."

7) The dealer then draws a card from those remaining face down on the table, and it is the turn of the player to the previous players' right.

8) As soon as one player has all three cards of a set, that set should be placed on the table beside their "owner."

9) Play continues in this manner until all cards are in sets on the table.

10) Each set in front of a player at the end of a game is worth two points, if they are correctly matched. Media specialist is to check this.

■ ■ ■

BALONEY

PURPOSE: To gain skill in recognizing IMC terminology.

GRADE LEVEL: Intermediate—4th grade through 6th grade

TIME: 25 minutes

NUMBER: Best played with a maximum of 16 students.

METHOD OF CHECKING: Self-checking

MATERIALS:
1)   16 sheets of 12x9" oak-tag board to form the "Baloney" board (shown
       below); 12 questions will be typed on each board. Four different boards
       (with a total of 48 different questions) will be needed to form a set
       (4 sets are needed). Number the boards in each set on the back (1-4)
       in order to keep sets together.

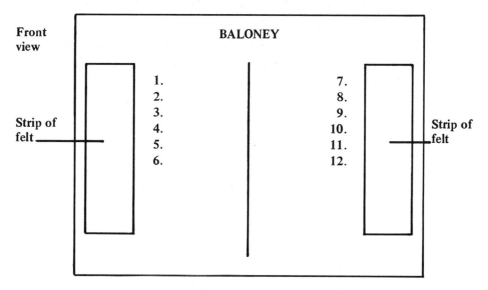

(Back view of "Baloney" board is shown on page 60)

Back view

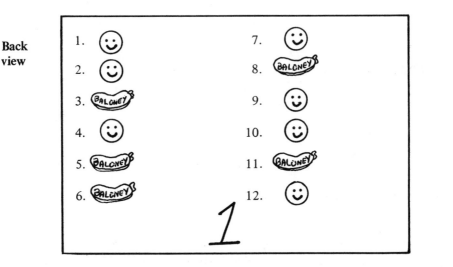

2) Sample statements to be answered "yes" (smile) or "no" (baloney):

Two main types of books in the IMC are fiction and easy. (baloney)

The call number is found on the spine of the book. (smile)

The name of a book is the title. (smile)

Fiction books have numbers and letters on the spine. (baloney)

The Dewey Decimal Classification System is a way of organizing books. (smile)

The person who writes a book is the illustrator. (baloney)

The index is in the back of a book. (smile)

An author can win a Caldecott Award. (baloney)

Books in the Dewey 500 section are science books. (smile)

Fiction books are arranged alphabetically by the author's last name. (smile)

A dictionary is a reference book. (smile)

The copyright date is the call number. (baloney)

IMC means Instructional Materials Center. (smile)

An author can win a Newbery Award. (smile)

Folklore and fairy tales are classified in the Dewey 300 section. (smile)

A glossary is a short dictionary found at the beginning of a book. (baloney)

The copyright date is the year the book was published. (smile)

Guide words are found both in a dictionary and an encyclopedia. (smile)

A collective biography is a work about the life of one person. (baloney)

A bibliography is a book containing a list of books on a specific subject. (smile)

A biography is shelved according to the name of the person being written about. (smile)

Readers' Guide to Periodical Literature is an index that helps a person locate articles in books. (baloney)

An author is the person who wrote the book or article. (smile)

Cards in the card catalog are filed alphabetically. (smile)

In the card catalog, there are four different types of cards—author, title, subject, and publisher. (baloney)

Cards in the card catalog are filed by the author, title, and subject in alphabetical order. (smile)

Subject cards in a card catalog are in capital letters and are usually typed in red. (smile)

An annotation is a short paragraph telling about a book. (smile)

3) Felt for both strips on the "Baloney" board (as shown) and for markers (smile faces for "yes," and baloneys for "no").

4) 16 6x9" envelopes in which to keep the smile faces and baloneys. (Determine how many of each per envelope according to the number of questions on the "Baloney" board.) Number the envelopes to correspond to the boards.

5) Large manila envelope (16x20") for the materials.

PROCEDURE:
1) Players sit around a set of tables in groups of four.

2) Pass out to each group a set of "Baloney" boards and a set of envelopes.

3) Each player is to read through the questions and answer them with a simple "yes" or "no"; as each question is answered, the player places a felt smile (to indicate "yes") or a felt baloney (to indicate "no") on the felt strips.

4) When each player finishes a "Baloney" board, the card can be turned over to self check.

(Procedures continue on page 62)

5)   The media specialist is to be available to answer questions and to see that players are honest in checking their answers.

6)   For each correct answer, the player scores a point.

7)   Players who finish a "Baloney" board and the self-checking should return the felt smiles and baloneys to their envelope and then trade boards and envelopes with someone else at that table who has finished.

8)   When two "Baloney" boards have been completed, the player may help someone else.

■ ■ ■

AUTHOR SCRAMBLE

PURPOSE: To acquire skill in alphabetizing authors' names—both one-letter alphabetizing and two-letter alphabetizing.

GRADE: Intermediate—4th grade

TIME: 25 minutes

NUMBER: Best played with a maximum of 16 students

METHOD OF CHECKING: Media specialist

MATERIALS:
1) 64 4x8" colored posterboard labels with author names printed on them in black felt tip pen; 16 cards per set for a total of 4 sets.

SET 1	SET 2
Aesop	Adrian, Mary
Aardema, Verna	Caney, Steven
Baker, Eugene	Carroll, Lewis
Farber, Norma	Folsom, Franklin
Hamilton, Virginia	Hawes, Judy
Jackson, Shirley	Joslin, Sesyle
Kastner, Erich	Kingman, Lee
Madison, Arnold	May, Julian
McGowen, Tom	Milgrom, Harry
Oliver, John	Orton, Helen
Renick, Marion	Ricciuti, Edward
Sasek, Miroslav	Simon, Norma
Urquhart, David	Vermeer, Jackie
Walsh, John	Warburg, Sandol
Wilson, Charles	Wohlrobe, Raymond
Zaffo, George	Zappler, Georg

(Sets 3 and 4 are on page 64)

SET 3	SET 4
Aliki	Augelli, John
Dickens, Charles	Barth, Edna
Eckert, Allan	Bliven, Bruce
Erdoes, Richard	Del Rey, Lester
Gag, Wanda	Enright, Elizabeth
Inouye, Carol	Gurney, Gene
Lampman, Evelyn	Ingrams, Doreen
Moody, Ralph	Ish-Kishor, Sulamith
Neurath, Marie	Jordan, June
Nourse, Alan	Lear, Edward
Parks, Aileen	Naden, Corinne
Quackenbush, Robert	Nyce, Vera
Taylor, Theodore	Podendorf, Illa
Webster, David	Taber, Gladys
Yolen, Jane	Unkelbach, Kurt
Yaroslavia	Wyler, Rose

2) 64 pieces of string or yarn to put through the tops of the author labels— 12" to 14" long, as they will slip over students' heads to hang on their chests.

3) Large manila envelope (12x15") for the materials.

PROCEDURE:

1) Divide the class into two evenly matched teams, and a leader is chosen for each.

2) Place author labels face down on a set of tables, around which students are gathered.

3) Each student chooses an author label, hangs it around his or her neck, and goes over to the team leader.

4) Once all students are gathered around the team leader, the media specialist shouts "go," and team members must place themselves in alphabetical order according to author's last name.

5) When the author labels are alphabetized, the team captain calls the media specialist over to check the team's work. If the team is correct, they go on to choose a second set of labels and proceed in the same manner.

6) If they are not correct, question the team as to why members placed themselves in that order. When they have answered to your satisfaction, work is to continue until all names are correctly alphabetized.

7) The team to alphabetize correctly all authors first wins the game.

8) If more practice is needed, start the procedure over, using a different set of author cards.

■ ■ ■

PURPOSE: To practice alphabetizing authors' names as they would appear on the spine of a book; to practice alphabetizing book titles.

GRADE LEVEL: 3rd and 4th grades

TIME: Form A–25 minutes
           Form B–25 minutes

NUMBER: Best played with a maximum of 16 students

METHOD OF CHECKING: Media specialist

MATERIALS:
1) Up to 182 3x10" book spines on colored posterboard, 12 to a pack (total number to be determined by the number of students playing at any one time; the figure 182 represents cards for 16 players). Suggested forms are below (for best results, use authors and titles found within your IMC); cut apart the "spines" and place in envelopes:

Margaret Sidney	Politi . . . The Butterflies Came	Walton	Tall Tales from the High Hills	JOHNNY BINGO	Uchida . . . The Promised Land
		* * *	Credle	■ ■ ■	
FIVE LITTLE PEPPERS		VOICES IN THE FOG		Norton	
Fic Sidney, Margaret	Fic Politi, Leo	Fic Walton, Elizabeth	Fic Credle, Ellis	Fic Norton, Browning	Fic Uchida, Yoskike
Grosset	Scribner's	Abelard	Hale	Coward	Harcourt

2)   Large manila envelope (16x20") for the materials.

PROCEDURE: Divide students into two evenly matched teams.

Form A

1)   Place packets of book spines face down on two tables. Each team is gathered around a table.

2)   Each student chooses a packet of book spines, takes it to a seat and proceeds to alphabetize the spines by the author's last name.

3)   When the spines are alphabetized, the student calls the media specialist over to check the work. If they are correct, that player may help someone else on the team. If they are not correct, the player continues to work until they are correctly alphabetized.

4)   The first team to correctly alphabetize all of the book spines in its packets wins the game.

Form B

1)   Same as Form A except teams have switched packets.

2)   Each student chooses a packet of book spines, takes it to a seat at a table and proceeds to alphabetize the spines by the title.

3)   Same as Form A.

4)   Same as Form A.

■ ■ ■

BOOK ALPHABETIZING

PURPOSE: To alphabetize actual books by the author's name and to shelve them with the collection on the shelves.

GRADE LEVEL: 3rd grade through 6th grade

TIME: 25 minutes

NUMBER: Best played with a maximum of 16 students (even number required here)

METHOD OF CHECKING: Media specialist

MATERIALS:
1) A stack of 12 books for every two students (total number to be determined by the number of students playing at any one time).

2) 2 bookends for every pair of students.

3) 12 colored strips (colored posterboard or paint chips) for every two students, one to be placed in each book.

PROCEDURE:
1) One stack of 12 books is placed on a flat surface for every two students participating.

2) Working in pairs, students alphabetize these, according to author's last name, between bookends.

3) When finished, students raise hands and the media specialist checks to see if the books are correctly alphabetized. If not correct, students continue work until they are correct.

4) If correct, the students involved attempt to shelve the books (alphabetically by author's last name) with the collection on the shelves. A colored strip juts out of each book thus shelved so the media specialist may check it.

5) For each stack correctly alphabetized the first time, students score two points; one point thereafter. For each book correctly shelved, each student receives one point.

■ ■ ■

PART II

DIPPING INTO THE DRAWER:
The Card Catalog

An IMC is for browsing. But when information is wanted, finding the right book by browsing may take too long. In addition to knowing how to select materials directly from the shelves or special collections, it is necessary to know how to use the card catalog, which is an index of each book in a library's collection. It enables library users to find any book or nonprint material quickly. It is a guidebook to the IMC.

Before using the games in this part, it would be wise to review with students how the card catalog is organized. The following filmstrips would be a good avenue to spark discussion:

1. "The Curious Case of the Card Catalog" (Adventures in Library Land; Educational Enrichment Materials; sound filmstrip; 15 minutes, color).

2. "The Card Catalog" (Your Library and Media Center: How to Get the Most from Them; The Center for Humanities, Inc.; sound filmstrip; 7 minutes; color).

3. "How to Use the Card Catalog" (Using the Elementary School Library; SVE; sound filmstrip; 16 minutes; color).

"C. C. WORM"

PURPOSE: To practice in locating the correct drawer in the card catalog in which
a title, author, or subject card should be located.

GRADE LEVEL: 3rd and 4th grades

TIME: 25 minutes

NUMBER: Best played with a maximum of 16 students

METHOD OF CHECKING: Answer sheet

MATERIALS:
1)   "C. C. Worm" ["Card Catalog Worm"] gameboard(s)—maximum of
four players to a board.

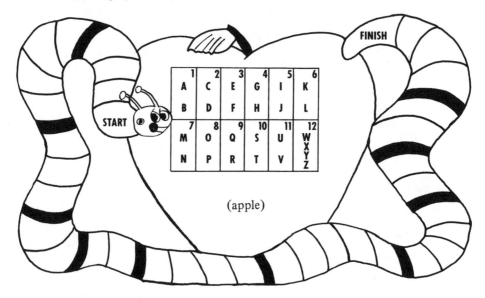

(apple)

2) 10 3x4" posterboard "blackout" cards, with "blackout" printed on one side and directions on the other side:

Go ahead 1 space	Go back 3 spaces
Go back 4 spaces	Go back 5 spaces
Lose 1 turn	Go ahead 2 spaces
Take an extra turn	Go back to start
Go ahead 1 space	Go back 6 spaces

3) 2 to 4 markers per gameboard—one for each player.

4) 75 3x4" colored posterboard cards—25 in each category—for title, author, and subject. Suggested entries for cards are below, but media specialists can choose items from their own collections:

Authors	Subjects
Bertha Hader	ACTING
Carolyn Haywood	BASEBALL—BIOGRAPHY
Phyllis Fenner	CACTUS
Herbert Zim	DINOSAURS
Elsa Beskow	EGG DECORATION
Joan Aiken	FLYING SAUCERS
Edna Chandler	GAMES—FICTION
Natalie Donna	HANDICRAFT
Sonia Gidal	INDIANS—LEGENDS
D. C. Ipsen	JAZZ MUSIC
Susan Jeffers	KNIGHTS AND KNIGHTHOOD
Alexander Keats	LIONS
Evelyn Lampman	MAGIC TRICKS
Patricia Martin	NONSENSE VERSES
Arden Newsome	PANDAS
Scott O'Dell	OUTER SPACE EXPLORATION
Ann Petry	RAILROADS
Seymour Reit	SCIENCE FICTION
Harvey Weiss	TREES—FICTION
Marilyn Sachs	UNDERWATER EXPLORATION
Sidney Taylor	VOYAGES AND TRAVELS
Janice Udry	WHALING—NEW ENGLAND HISTORY
Paul Villiard	YELLOWSTONE NATIONAL PARK
Carol York	ZOOLOGY
Maurice Sendak	WITCHCRAFT—FICTION

(List of Titles appears on page 72)

Titles

Safety Can Be Fun	Games in the Street
Zoo Doctor	Hunting of the Snark
Kickapoo	Incident on Hawks Hill
Manners Can Be Fun	Last Horse on the Sands
Caddie Woodlawn	Papermakers
Up a Crooked River	Over Sea under Stone
Peter's Pinto	Secret Agent on Flight 101
True Zoo Stories	Quips and Quirks
ABCs of Origami	Ramona the Pest
Beaver Pond	Viking Explorers
Doctor J	The Warlock of Westfall
Easy Crafts Book	Young Grizzly
Fire Bringer	

5) Make a master answer sheet for each gameboard using the above lists and add the correct answer for each.

6) Large manila envelope (16x20") for the materials.

PROCEDURE:

1) All players place markers on "start."

2) Title, author, and subject cards are shuffled and placed face down on the apple on the gameboard.

3) "Blackout" cards are shuffled and placed face down next to the title, author, and subject cards on the gameboard.

4) Players take turns in alphabetical order by last names, with the person whose name starts with the letter closest to the beginning of the alphabet going first. Play goes clockwise around the table.

5) The first player draws a "category" (subject, author, title) card and tells what drawer to look in to find the information.

6) If correct, the player moves the number of spaces indicated on that card catalog drawer and places his card at the bottom of the original pile of "category" cards.

7) If a player lands on a black space, that person must draw a "blackout" card and follow the directions on it.

8) The blackout card is then returned to the bottom of the pile, and play passes to the next person.

9) All other players take turns following the same procedure.

10) The first person to reach "finish" wins.

■ ■ ■

PURPOSE: To give practice in using the alphabetical guide labels on the outside of card catalog drawers.

GRADE LEVEL: Primary—3rd grade

TIME: 35 minutes

NUMBER: Best played with a maximum of 16 students

METHOD OF CHECKING: Media specialist

MATERIALS:
1) 2 dice.

2) Cardboard box (30x30"—large) with "drawers" drawn on one side and a 3½" long slot cut into each one:

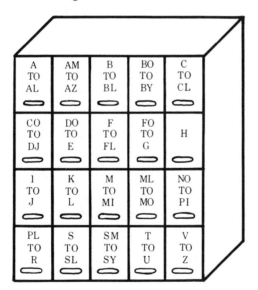

A TO AL	AM TO AZ	B TO BL	BO TO BY	C TO CL
CO TO DJ	DO TO E	F TO FL	FO TO G	H
I TO J	K TO L	M TO MI	ML TO MO	NO TO PI
PL TO R	S TO SL	SM TO SY	T TO U	V TO Z

(For best results, use the lettering that applies to your catalog drawers.)

(Materials list continues on page 74)

3) 48 3x4" colored posterboard cards with an author, subject, or title printed on each of them.

Authors	Subjects
K. M. Briggs	MAPS
Helen Cresswell	OLYMPIC GAMES
Jane Curry	PANDAS
Peter Dickinson	ROCKS
William Katz	MAGIC—FICTION
Mollie Hunter	FAIRIES—FICTION
Robert Leckie	PREJUDICES—FICTION
Edith McCall	MYSTERY & DETECTIVE STORIES
William Mayne	SUPERNATURAL—FICTION
Doris Orgel	WOLVES—FICTION
Leo Politi	SCOTLAND—FICTION
Winifred Madison	UNITED STATES—HISTORY— REVOLUTION, 1775-1783
Anne Rockwell	BIRDS—NORTH AMERICA
Millicent Selsam	BASKETBALL—BIOGRAPHY
Tobi Tobias	FOOTBALL—BIOGRAPHY
Louis Untermeyer	TENNIS—BIOGRAPHY

Titles

Alligator Pie	Sea Turtles
Bedtime for Frances	Virginia Colony
Mirror of Danger	Walking Stones
Nine Planets	The Witch of Blackbird Pond
On City Streets	Yertle the Turtle
Pioneers of Rocketry	The Party That Lasted All Summer
Quitting Deal	Hobberdy Dick
Red Fairy Book	Earthfasts

4) Large manila envelope (10x13") for the materials.

PROCEDURE:

1) Before the students arrive, place the cardboard box with "drawers" drawn on one side and the author, title, and subject cards on a table. Cards are to be face down.

2) Divide the students into two evenly matched teams, and choose a leader for each.

3) Each team will group themselves in front of the cardboard box and cards.

4) Players are to arrange themselves in alphabetical order, by last name, behind the team leader.

5) Provide 1 die to each team leader, who then throws the die for a number. The team with the highest number gets the first turn.

6) The leader chooses a card from the pile, and then drops the card into the appropriate slot and tells why it belongs in that drawer. All the cards will fall into the bottom of the large box, to be retrieved at the end of the game.

7) If the card is correctly placed and the appropriate reason is given, the team scores a point. If not, the opposing team automatically scores a point, and then takes an additional turn.

8) Media specialist makes sure that the appropriate reason is given for placement of card.

9) Play alternates between the two teams until everyone has had a chance to play two times.

10) Team with the most points wins.

■ ■ ■

"C. C. SPREE"

PURPOSE: To practice locating the correct drawer in the card catalog from an author, title, or subject card.

GRADE LEVEL: 3rd and 4th grades

TIME: 25 minutes

NUMBER: Best played with a maximum of 16 students

METHOD OF CHECKING: Answer sheet

MATERIALS:
1) 8 9x12" tag-board "C. C. Spree" ["Card Catalog Spree"] gameboards (marked with the lettering that corresponds to your catalog drawers), maximum of 2 students per gameboard:

A to Al	Am to Az	B to Bl	Bo to By	C to Cl	Co to Dj	Do to E
F to Fo	Fr to G	H	I to J	K to L	M to Mi	Mo to N
O to Pi	Pl to R	S to Sl	Sm to Sy	T to U	V to Wh	Wi to Z

2) 336 2x2" colored posterboard cards (168 yellow, 168 orange). Divide the cards into 8 single-color sets of 42 cards each. Mark each card with a name, title, or subject—best results being gained by using those found in your card catalog. Number the cards on the back to indicate the set (1-8):

SET 1

Roz Abisch	Edith McCall
ABRAHAM LINCOLN	MACHINERY
Esther Averill	F. N. Monjo
AMERICA	MODELING
Babbis Baastad	Graham Oakley
BABIES—FICTION	OCEAN
David Boehm	Marian Place
BOATS AND BOATING	PLANETS
John C. Caldwell	James Razzi
CABLES	RABBITS—FICTION
Belle Coates	Helga Sandberg
COAST GUARD	SANTA CLAUS—PICTURES
Arnold Dobrin	Beatrice Smith
DOGS—FICTION	SNAKES
Walter C. Fabel	Mark Taylor
FABLES	TAHITI
Ruth Franchere	STATE BIRDS
FRANCE—FICTION	Space Cat and the Kittens
Berta Hader	TOADS
HAIKU	Today in Old Boston
Tom Ingram	Judy Varga

3) 48 2x2" colored posterboard cards (24 each of yellow and orange), with 24 of each color-marked as follows:

8 "spree" (free card), 8 "lose 1 turn," and 8 "take 2 turns."

Form 8 sets, each containing one card each of the three kinds here; add one of these to each of the sets in number (2), keeping colors in these combined sets (45 cards total) the same.

4) Make master answer sheets for each full set (cards from numbers 2 and 3), listing the authors, titles, and subjects, and the drawers in which they belong (using the same initials as appear on the gameboard).

5) Large manila envelope (12x15") for the materials.

PROCEDURE:

1) Players are divided into pairs and given a "C. C. Spree" gameboard and a set of cards (45 cards in all, per set).

2) Cards in each 45 card set are shuffled and placed face down in front of the players in two piles near the "Spree" gameboard. One player has yellow cards and the other has orange cards.

3) Each player takes turns drawing a card from his or her set until a "Spree" card turns up. This indicates the player who begins the game.

(Procedures continue on page 78)

4) Cards are then reshuffled and placed on the table face down beside the gameboard.

5) The first player draws a card and determines on which card catalog drawer it belongs.

6) If the decision is correct, the card remains on the drawer. If it is incorrect, the card is returned to the bottom of the pile and the turn goes to the other player.

7) Players are to check each other, refer to answer sheets, and if a question arises, call the media specialist over.

8) If a player draws a card that belongs on a drawer where a card has already been placed, that player must return the card to the bottom of the pile and lose that turn.

9) A "Spree" card may be used as a wild card and placed on any drawer.

10) Players are to follow the directions printed on the cards if they draw a "take 2 turns" or "lose 1 turn" card.

11) The player who correctly places the most cards is the winner, but each player scores one point for each card correctly placed.

■ ■ ■

"C. C. SORT"

PURPOSE: To gain skill in differentiating among author cards, title cards, and subject cards.

GRADE LEVEL: Primary—3rd grade

TIME: 25 minutes

NUMBER: Best played with a maximum of 16 students

METHOD OF CHECKING: Media specialist

MATERIALS:
1) 6 4x10" colored posterboard labels; two each will be lettered "Author," "Title," or "Subject," to form 2 sets.

2) Masking tape.

3) 100 old card catalog ["c. c."] cards, divided into 2 packs. A pack consists of different author, title, and subject cards, but does not necessarily contain complete cards for each book.

4) Large manila envelope (10x13") for the materials.

PROCEDURE:
1) Divide the students into two evenly matched teams, and choose a leader for each.

2) Tape a set of labels on each of two tables (as below) and place catalog cards face down on the tables near the labels.

   [AUTHOR]   [TITLE]   [SUBJECT]

3) Each team is assigned a table.

4) Team members line up behind the leader, who then steps to the other side of the table and becomes the officiator.

5) Each team member, in turn, draws a card and places it on the category label to which it belongs.

(Procedures continue on page 80)

6) The leader checks to see if all the cards are placed correctly. However, during play, the leader cannot correct a card. When all are used, the leader checks and corrects any cards that are incorrectly placed.

7) When the leader feels that all cards are placed correctly, that person raises a hand. The media specialist will then check the categories.

8) If the cards are correctly placed, the team is finished. If some cards are incorrectly placed, the media specialist removes them from the categories and asks for volunteers to place them again.

9) One point is given for each card correctly placed, and the winning team scores two extra points.

■ ■ ■

"C. C. FLASH"

PURPOSE: To gain practice in differentiating among author, title, and subject cards.

GRADE LEVEL: 3rd grade through 6th grade

TIME: 25 minutes

NUMBER: Best played with a maximum of 16 students.

METHOD OF CHECKING: Media specialist

MATERIALS:
1) 1 opaque projector.
2) Screen.
3) 32 old catalog cards.
4) 1 die.
5) Large manila envelope (10x13") for the materials.

PROCEDURE:
1) The group is divided into two teams.
2) The teams form two lines and sit facing the screen.
3) The first person of each team rolls the die to determine the starting team. Thereafter, teams alternate turns.
4) The media specialist puts one card into the opaque projector and flashes the card onto the screen.
5) The first student of the starting team must identify the type of card (author, title, or subject).
6) If correct, a point is scored for that team.
7) If incorrect, the other team has a chance to gain a point by answering correctly.
8) Play continues on the first card, alternating teams, until one team can answer correctly and score a point.
9) Media specialist continues with the rest of the cards in the same manner.
10) The team with the most points wins.

■ ■ ■

SNAP BACK

PURPOSE: To gain practice using guide cards in the card catalog.

GRADE LEVEL: 3rd grade through 6th grade

TIME: 25 minutes

NUMBER: Best played with a maximum of 16 students.

METHOD OF CHECKING: Answer sheet

MATERIALS:
1)   4 "Snap Back" gameboards (or however many will be needed)—
16x12" colored posterboard gameboards divided into squares
1½x1½"; maximum of 4 players per gameboard.

(The snap back area looks better with a contrasting color of posterboard glued to the center.)

2)   4 markers per gameboard—one for each player.

3)   One cloth sack per gameboard in which to keep markers.

4)   a)   240 3x4" colored posterboard cards—80 in each of the
categories, title, author, and subject. Divide into 4 sets of 60
cards each (20 from each category).

b)   Each card should have a number from 1 to 5 in the left-hand
corner to indicate the number of spaces to move when the
correct answer is given. Numbers are to be chosen at random.

[Suggested authors, title, and subjects appear on page 83,
below sample of gameboard.]

SNAP BACK GAMEBOARD

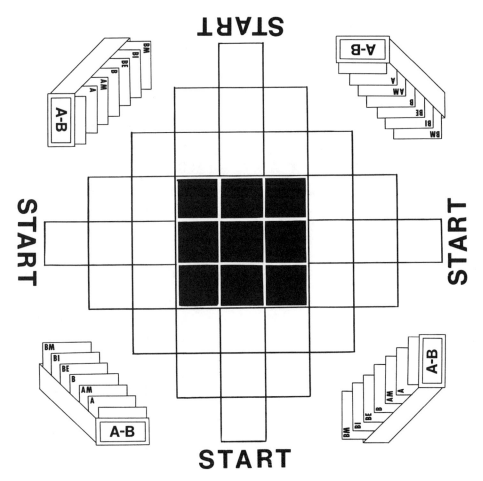

Suggested authors, titles, and subjects:

A-AM

A for the Ark
About Helpers Who Work at Night
Adams, Ruth
Adelaide
All Ready for Winter
Adler, Irving
AFRICA
AIR

AM-AZ

America's Best Loved Wild Animals
Anatole
Andersen, Hans Christian
Angelo, the Naughty One
Angus and the Ducks
ANTS
Arbuthnot, May Hill
Ardizzone, Edward

(Listings continue on page 84)

A-AM (cont'd)

ALASKA
Albert the Albatross
ALLIGATORS
Alphabet Book

AM-AZ (cont'd)

ARIZONA
ASTRONOMY
AZTECS
APES

B-BE

Bad Boy, Good Boy
Barr, Jane
BASEBALL
BASKETBALL
Bate, Norman
Babar and the Wully Wully
BATS—FICTION
Bad Bear
Bach, Alice
Bacon, Peggy
BACTERIA
Baby Animal Book

BE-BI

Be a Frog, a Bird, or a Tree
Bear on a Motorcycle
BEAVERS
Beatty, Jerome
Bedtime for Frances
Beim, Jerrold
Ben and Me
Bemelmans, Ludwig
Beanie
Beezus and Ramona
BEES
Beat the Turtle Drum

BI-BM

Big Ball of String
Big Snow
BIRDS
Birthday Boy
Bishop, Claire
BISON
Bitter, Gary
BIRTHSTONES
Bishop, Ann
Black Fairy Tales
Black Stallion Returns
Bleeker, Sonia

BM-BZ

BONES
Book of Giants
Bowman, Kathleen
BOY SCOUTS
Brandenberg, Franz
Bread and Jam for Frances
Brown, Margaret Wise
Bulla, Clyde Robert
BUNYAN, PAUL
Burchard, Marshall
Burton, Virginia Lee
BUTTERFLIES

5)   Master list of guide cards and the authors, titles, and subjects that are on them—one for each gameboard to use as an answer sheet; dry-mounted to a piece of colored posterboard.

6)   Large manila envelope (12x15") for the materials.

PROCEDURE:

1) Students count off in fours and divide into groups around tables.

2) Each group is given a "Snap Back" gameboard, markers in sack, cards, and answer key (which is placed face down in the center of the table beside the gameboard).

3) The student whose last name is closest to the beginning of the alphabet starts the game. Play continues clockwise.

4) The players each place one marker at "start."

5) The player who gets the first turn becomes the dealer, shuffles the cards, and deals all of them out to the players.

6) Each player places the dealt cards in a pile face down on the table in front of himself.

7) The first player draws a card from his pile and tells between which two guide cards on the board that title, author, or subject would be found. If the player's reply is correct, that person moves the number of spaces indicated in the left-hand corner of the card. The card is then placed face up next to that player's pile, making a discard pile.

8) If the other players are not sure that a reply is correct, they may check the answer sheet.

9) If the answer is incorrect, the player does not move the marker and places the card at the bottom of the "play" pile.

10) The player may move the marker in any direction except backwards, with the object of reaching the opposite start position.

11) If only one player reaches the "Snap Back" (blacked-out) area, that person may remain until another player lands there.

12) When a second player lands in the "Snap Back" area, the first one must "snap back" to the "start" position. Only one player at a time (the most recent arrival) is allowed to occupy the "Snap Back" area.

13) Players may choose to go around the "Snap Back" area to avoid being sent back to "start." (Refer to gameboard.)

14) If all of the snapback cards are used and no player has reached the goal, the discard piles are shuffled together and the dealer deals a different set of cards to each player.

15) The player who first reaches the goal wins.

16) Each player is to keep track of the number of personal correct answers. For each correct answer, that player scores one point.

■   ■   ■

"C. C. PUZZLE"

PURPOSE: To gain practice in locating author, title, and subject cards in the card catalog.

GRADE LEVEL: Primary—3rd grade

TIME: 25 minutes for each form (A, B, or C)

NUMBER: Best played with a maximum of 16 students

METHOD OF CHECKING: Media specialist

MATERIALS:
1) 16 9x12" tag-board "C. C. Puzzle" ["Card Catalog Puzzle"] cards, as in the following. For best results, use different subjects for each group of four students.

	R	E	A	D	I	N	G
SCIENCE							
POETRY							
BEARS—FICTION							
CHRISTMAS—FICTION							
FANTASY							
HALLOWEEN							

2) 16 Vis-a-Vis® pens.

3) Damp paper towels to wipe off the marks from "C. C. Puzzle" cards when game is finished.

4) Card catalog drawers.

5)   Large manila envelope (12x15") for the materials.

PROCEDURE:

Form A

1)   Before the students arrive, arrange the card catalog drawers on tables or flat surfaces around the room.

2)   Each individual player is given both a "C. C. Puzzle" card and a Vis-a-Vis® pen.

3)   The players may search the card catalog drawers to find a title for each category, beginning with each letter at the top of the columns.

4)   Ten points will be given for each title listed.

5)   The player with the highest number of points is the winner. Each player, however, does earn the number of points personally scored.

Form B

1)   Step 1 is the same as Form A.

2)   The players are divided into four groups of four each.

3)   Each group is given both a "C. C. Puzzle" card and a Vis-a-Vis® pen.

4)   Each group is to search the card catalog drawers to find a title for each category, beginning with each letter at the top of the column.

5)   Ten points will be given for each title listed.

6)   The group with the highest number of points wins. Each group, however, does earn the number of points that it scores.

Form C

The game may be played as in Form A and Form B, except that the books' authors are listed for each category instead of the book titles.

■ ■ ■

UNSCRAMBLE US

PURPOSE: To demonstrate the ability to locate library materials in the card catalog by author or title.

GRADE LEVEL: 3rd and 4th grades

TIME: 25 minutes

NUMBER: Best played with a maximum of 16 students

METHOD OF CHECKING: Media specialist

MATERIALS:

1) 32 Caldecott-winner book jackets mounted on heavy cardboard or colored posterboard. (On the back, draw various irregular shapes in preparation for jigsaw puzzle-type cutting. Give each book jacket a number, then number each cut-out shape as belonging to one puzzle.) Laminate and then cut the jackets into various pieces to make the jigsaw puzzle.

2) 32 6x9" manila envelopes to keep the puzzle pieces in, each envelope to be marked with the book title and author. In the lower right-hand corner, place the number for that particular puzzle.

3) Type or letter on 4½x6" oak-tag cards or dittoed "problem sheets." On a separate piece of paper, write the following information:

Student's Name	Author:
Title:	Call Number:
Copyright Date:	Publisher:
The above information is to be found in the CARD CATALOG. You may not be able to find all the information, but do the best you can.	

4) When a student has finished the first puzzle and problem sheet, the drawer is returned to the card catalog and a second puzzle can be chosen. Two puzzles are a good number for this game.

■ ■ ■

CATA KEY

PURPOSE: To practice using the card catalog in order to locate author, title, and subject cards.

GRADE LEVEL: Primary—3rd grade

TIME: 25 minutes

NUMBER: Best played with a maximum of 16 students

METHOD OF CHECKING: Media specialist

MATERIALS:

1) Card catalog drawers.

2) 32 colored oak-tag board or posterboard keys (2 keys are needed for each student).

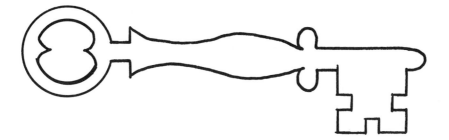

3) 75 3x4" colored posterboard cards—25 marked in each category (author, title, and subject), using either the lists found in "C. C. Worm," page 70, or cards made up according to the information found within your own card catalog.

4) Call slips and pencils for each student.

5) Large manila envelope (10x13") for the materials.

PROCEDURE:

1) Cardboard keys are placed in book pockets or on shelves where materials would be found, before class time.

2) Before the students arrive, arrange the card catalog drawers around the room along with call slips and pencils.

3) Divide the students into two evenly matched teams, and choose a leader for each.

4) Each person on a team chooses a poster board card: decides whether it is an author, title, or subject card; hunts around the room for the appropriate card catalog drawer; and looks up the necessary information in that drawer.

5) Once the catalog card has been found, the player is to write on the call slip the complete author, title, and call number.

6) From here, the player goes to the shelves, locates the material and finds the key that is either in the book pocket or near the materials.

7) When a key is found, the player gives it to the team leader and chooses another card with which to follow the same procedure.

8) When one book and one non-print item have been found by a player and two keys located and given to the team leader, the player may help someone else on the team.

9) The team with the most points (keys) at the end of the period is declared the winner.

■ ■ ■

PURPOSE: To develop accuracy and skill in locating IMC materials and in using the card catalog.

GRADE LEVEL: Primary—3rd grade

TIME: 25 minutes

NUMBER: Best played with a maximum of 16 students

METHOD OF CHECKING: Media specialist

MATERIALS:
1)   Card catalog drawers.
2)   188 3x4" problem cards cut from colored posterboard or construction paper (40 labeled with a subject; 40, title; 40, author; 46, locating books [one-half easy fiction and one-half regular fiction] ; 22, locating Dewey):

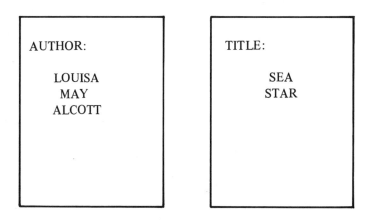

(Samples of problem cards continue on page 92)

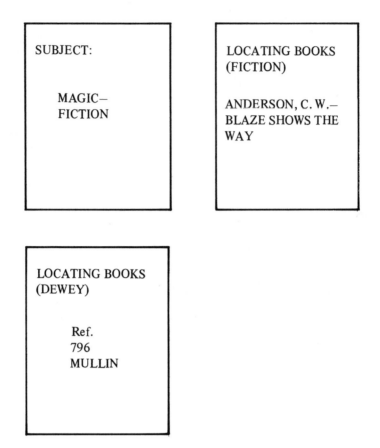

SUBJECT:

MAGIC—
FICTION

LOCATING BOOKS
(FICTION)

ANDERSON, C. W.—
BLAZE SHOWS THE
WAY

LOCATING BOOKS
(DEWEY)

Ref.
796
MULLIN

Suggested titles, subjects, and "location" lists follow:

Titles	Subjects
Cat Who Wishes to Be a Man	AUSTRALIA—FICTION
Fabulous Firework Family	EGYPT—FICTION
Where the Wild Things Are	SCHOOL—FICTION
Brownie Makes the Headlines	PHILADELPHIA—HISTORY
Invisible Snow	FRANCE—FICTION
Sea Star	NEWBERY MEDAL AWARDS
Madeline and the Gypsies	HISTORY, ANCIENT
Coll and His White Pig	EUROPEAN WAR, 1914-1918
Baba Yaga's Secret	COOKERY
Curious George Rides a Bike	JUNGLE—FICTION
Tale of the Faithful Dove	DICTIONARIES
King George's Head Was Made of Lead	ISLANDS OF THE PACIFIC—FICTION
Alexander and the Wind-Up Mouse	CHRISTMAS STORIES

Titles (cont'd)	Subjects (cont'd)
Song of the Swallows	GHOST STORIES
Old Dame Trot and Her Comical Cat	BRONZE AGE–FICTION
Drums, Rattles and Bells	BABY ELEPHANTS
Book of Three	MICE–FICTION
Blue Bird	NAVAHO INDIANS–FICTION
Hobbit	ZOOS–FICTION
Fiesta Time in Mexico	QUAILS–FICTION
Animal Babies	U. S. CONSTITUTION
History of Body Armor	BOOKBINDING
Arrow to the Sun	PAPIER-MACHE
Eddie and the Fire Engine	ANIMALS–HABITS AND BEHAVIOR
Who Is Victoria?	BEARS–FICTION
Abominable Swamp Man	MAGIC–FICTION
Lazy Bear	LAPLAND–FICTION
Wait Till the Moon Is Full	TEXAS–FICTION
Sam's First Fish	CALDECOTT MEDAL AWARDS
Phantom Toolbooth	FOLKLORE–AFRICA
Quest of Archimedes	SUPERNATURAL–FICTION
Ten Apples Up on Top	CAT–FICTION
Sparrow Socks	RAILROADS
Round Trip for Johnny	FANTASIES
Mistletoe: Fact and Folklore	WITCHCRAFT–FICTION
Chanticleer and the Fox	HALLOWEEN–FICTION
Gabbit, the Magic Rabbit	STORIES IN RHYME
Piggy in the Puddle	SANTA CLAUS–FICTION
Night Noises and Other Mole and	WINTER–FICTION
Troll Stories	FABLES
Freddy Plays Football	LIONS–FICTION
Joan of Arc	

Locating Books–Fiction

Alcott–Little Women
Zolotow–Mr. Rabbit and the Lovely
  Present
Gauch–This Time Tempe Wick
Corbett–Case of the Silver Skull
Cooper, Susan–The Grey King
Fatio–Hector Penguin
Farley–Black Stallion
Jeschke–Fire Rose

Locating Books–Dewey

299–Baker, Betty
794.1–Leeming, Joseph
709.98–Glubok, Shirley
398.4–Manning-Sanders
Bio–Jemison, Mary
Bio–Jefferson, Thomas
917.48–Hall, Elvajean
978–Burt, Olive
220–Turner, Philip

("Location" lists continue on page 94)

Locating Books—Fiction (cont'd)

Haywood, Carolyn—Eddie and Louella
Duvoisin—Periwinkle
McCloskey—Homer Price
Peet, Bill—Spooky Tail of Prewitt
 Peacock
Warner, Gertrude—Boxcar Children
Keene—Witch Tree Symbol
Rey—Curious George Goes to
 the Hospital
Mayer, Mercer—Mrs. Beggs and the
 Wizard
Tudor—Corgiville Fair
Waber—Lyle, Lyle Crocodile
Haley—Abominable Swamp Man
Anderson, C. W.—Blaze Shows the
 Way
Travers—Mary Poppins
Schulz, Charles—Charlie Brown's
 Christmas
Estes—Witch Family
Clemens—Adventures of Tom
 Sawyer
Lawson, Robert—Ben and Me
Eager—Half Magic
Todd—Space Cat and the Kittens
Peck, Robert—Rabbits and Redcoats
Sendak—Where the Wild Things Are
Dixon—Secret Warning

Locating Books—Dewey (cont'd)

550—Epstein, Samuel
330—Riedel, Manfred
970.3—Conklin, Paul
738—Fisher, Leonard
574.5—Headly, Eleanor
133.4—Starkey, Marion
910.4—Murphy, Barbara
808.81—Tripp, Wallace
808.87—Keller, Charles
808.8H—Cantwell, Mary
Bio—Jackson, Mahalia
821—Lear, Edward
170—Leaf, Munro
001—Liss, Howard
Ref. 301.2—National Geographic
529—Adler, Irving
970.1—Gridley, Marion
680—Yates, Brock
598—Ozone, Lucy
Ref. 796—Mullin
920 Bio—Fleming
614.8—Tamarin, Alfred
793.7—Fletcher, Helen
440—Joslin, Sesyle
611—Schuman, Benjamin
745.5—D'Amato, Janet
Ref. 808.88—Bartlett
918.3—Carpenter, Allan
808.82—Korty, Carol

Authors

Louisa May Alcott
Lloyd Alexander
Clarence Anderson
Jerrold Beim
Frank Bonham
Jean Bothwell
Carol Carrick
Carroll Colby
Roald Dahl
Edward Edelson

Authors (cont'd)

Walter Farley
James Flora
Shirley Glubok
Jane Goodsell
Langston Hughes
Will James
Margaret Johnson
Rudyard Kipling
Eleanor Lattimore
Lois Lenski
Clive Staples Lewis
George Mendoza
Misha Miles
Alan Milne
Mary Norton
William Peet
Glen Rounds
Louis Slobodkin
William Steig
Alfred H. Tamarin
Marguerite Walters
Laura I. Wilder
Herbert Zim

3) 4x6" oak-tag instruction cards or dittoed sheets; reason for each exercise is printed on the instruction card.

a) AUTHOR:

Does the IMC have any books written by the author named on the card in front of you?

If so, write the call number and the title of one book *by*, not about, the author on a piece of paper.

AUTHOR: _____

CALL NUMBER:

TITLE: _____   _____

(Sample cards continue on page 96)

b) SUBJECT HEADINGS:

Does the IMC have any books about the subject card in front of you?

If so, write the subject, author, title and call number of one book, on the subject, on a piece of paper:

SUBJECT: _____

TITLE: _____

AUTHOR: _____

CALL NUMBER: _____

c) TITLE:

Does the IMC have the title written on the card in front of you?

If so, write the title, author, and call number of the book on a piece of paper.

TITLE: _____

CALL NUMBER:

AUTHOR: _____

d) LOCATING BOOKS: FICTION AND NON-FICTION

The FICTION card, in front of you, gives the author's last name as well as a book title. Find the book in the card catalog. Go to the shelf and bring it to the media specialist and/or aide to be checked.

The DEWEY card gives a call number as well as the author's name. Locate the book bearing this information on the shelf and bring it to the media specialist and/or aide to be checked.

4) Large manila envelope (12x15") for the materials.

PROCEDURE:

1) Students receive a problem card from one category as well as the appropriate instruction card or sheet, and read the instructions. Then students go to the card catalog and take the appropriate drawer in which to find the information.

2) When a student has solved the problem, the drawer is returned to the card catalog and another problem card is selected, along with the appropriate instructions. At least three cards in each category should be completed to demonstrate the ability to find the needed information.

3) When three problem cards have been completed, the media specialist checks the work. The student can then be given a different instruction card and proceed as above (Steps 1 and 2).

4) Four points are to be given for each correctly answered problem card.

■   ■   ■

SCAVENGER HUNT

PURPOSE: To develop skill in locating author, title, and subject cards in the card catalog.

GRADE LEVEL: 3rd and 4th grades

TIME: 25 minutes

NUMBER: Best played with a maximum of 16 students

METHOD OF CHECKING: Media specialist

MATERIALS:
1) Card catalog drawers.
2) 32 3½x3½" colored posterboard clue cards. Only questions should be typed or lettered on the cards.

> This man was the first president of the United States. (George Washington)
>
> A. A. Milne wrote many books about a little bear who loved honey; who is this bear? (Winnie-the-Pooh)
>
> October 31st is the day to celebrate this scarey holiday. (Halloween)
>
> Under what subject would you look for a book on curses, hexes, and spells? (Witchcraft)
>
> This man was the sixteenth president of the United States. (Abraham Lincoln)
>
> This young girl had a wicked stepmother and two wicked step-sisters. (Cinderella)
>
> February 14th is the day to celebrate this holiday for friends and lovers. (Valentine's Day)
>
> Who is the red-suited man associated with the Christmas season? (Santa Claus)
>
> Under what subject would you look for a book of recipes? (Cookery)
>
> This author wrote many books about a beautiful black stallion. (Walter Farley)
>
> What holiday is associated with bunnies and egg hunts? (Easter)

At a birth celebration of a young princess, all of the fairies of the realm were present except one. (Sleeping Beauty)

Susan Lee is the author of many books on the American Revolution; find one.

Name the series of mystery books in which two brothers solve all of the cases. (Hardy Boys)

This author wrote a series of books about her frontier life as a child. (Laura Ingalls Wilder)

H. Rey wrote several books about a curious monkey. What is the monkey's name? (Curious George)

This author wrote a book about Jesse Owens, a black athlete who won four gold medals in the 1936 Olympics. (Paul G. Neimark)

Ludwig Bemelmans wrote several books about a little French girl; name her. (Madeline, etc.)

Name one book about the inventor of the telephone. (*Mr. Bell Invents the Telephone; Aleck Bell, Ingenious Boy*)

Name the author of the *Bear's Nature Guide.* (Berenstain)

Michael Bond wrote a series of books about a bear who was always getting into trouble; what is the bear's name? (Paddington)

George Franklin wrote a book about an elk; name the book. (*Rocky the Bull Elk*)

Name the author of the book claiming to be "an inside story" of the FBI. (John Joseph Floherty)

Name a fairy tale written by Frances Browne. (*Granny's Wonderful Chair*)

Glen Rounds wrote a book about American Indians; name the book. (*Buffalo Harvest*)

Who is the author of a series of books about women and how they can be employed? (Gloria Goldreich)

Name the man written about in *We Shall Live in Peace.* (Martin Luther King)

Who is the author of the story about a rabbit named Peter? (Beatrix Potter)

Under what subject would you find a book about "knock, knocks"? (Jokes)

Who is the author of the book about a mouse who rides a motorcycle? (Beverly Cleary)

(List continues on page 100)

Name the author of a series of science fiction stories about the TV
series "Star Trek" (numbered 1 through 10). (James Blish)

3) Master list of clues and answers for the use of the media specialist.

4) Call slips and pencils for each student.

5) "Parchment" awards—game award certificates made from colored
paper.

6) Large manila envelope (10x13") for the materials.

PROCEDURE:

1) Before the students arrive, arrange the card catalog drawers around the
room along with call slips and pencils.

2) Divide the students into two evenly matched teams.

3) Place two clue cards for each team member on a table around which
team members have gathered.

4) The media specialist reminds players that non-print material can be
included.

5) Members of the team discuss under what subject they are to look in
the card catalog by determining what the clues mean. Once the subjects
have been determined and a list made, 1) they check with the media
specialist to see that they are correct, and 2) each team member takes
two subjects and hunts around the room for the appropriate card catalog drawer in which to look up the clue.

6) Once the subject card has been found, the player writes on the call
slip the author, title, and call number of the item involved.

7) The player goes to the shelves, locates the material, and brings it back
to the team table. If the material is not on the shelf, the media
specialist checks the fact with the player and places the call slip on
the table in lieu of the item.

8) The team to find all of their books or non-print material first will be
declared winners of the hunt and will receive a "parchment" to take
back to their rooms.

■ ■ ■

PURPOSE: To practice locating the correct drawer in the card catalog from an author, title, or subject card.

GRADE LEVEL: Intermediate—4th grade through 6th grade

TIME: 25 minutes

NUMBER: Best played with a maximum of 16 students

METHOD OF CHECKING: Answer sheet

MATERIALS:

1) 4 20x14" gameboards [see page 102 for sample of board], or one for every group of no more than 4 students.

2) 90 3½x3½" colored posterboard cards: 30 author, 30 title, and 30 subject.

Authors	Subjects
Irving Adler	ANIMALS—FICTION
Glen Balch	BALLET
Eric Carle	CATS
Roald Dahl	DEATH—FICTION
Edward Dolch	EARTHQUAKES
Allan Eckert	EXTINCT ANIMALS
Doris Faber	FAIRY TALES
Sonia Gidal	GAMES
Gail Haley	HAIKU
Carol Inouye	INSECTS
Linda Jacobs	INDIANS OF NORTH AMERICA—
Virginia Kahl	FICTION
Phyllis LaFarge	KARTING—FICTION
Ruth Manning-Sanders	LEAVES
Avery Nagle	MAGIC TRICKS
Alan Nourse	NONSENSE BOOKS
Graham Oakley	NURSERY RHYMES
Rodney Peppe	OCEANOGRAPHY
Edward Radlauer	PAPIER-MACHE

(List continues on page 103)

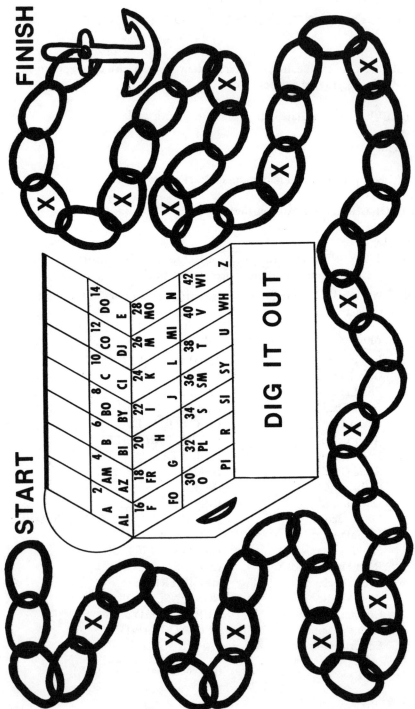

FINISH

START

2	4	6	8	10	12	14
AM	B	BO	C	CO	DJ	DO
AZ	BI	BY	CI			
A						
AL						

16	18	20	22	24	26	28
F	FR	H	I	K	M	MO
FO	G		J	L	MI	E
						N

30	32	34	36	38	40	42
O	PL	S	SM	T	V	WI
PI	R	SI	SY	U	WH	Z

DIG IT OUT

Authors (cont'd)	Subjects (cont'd)
Marilyn Sachs	RIDDLES
Gladys Taber	SPACE AND TIME—FICTION
Janice Udry	TALL TALES
Jules Verne	UNIDENTIFIED FLYING OBJECTS
Daisy Wallace	VOLCANOES
John Yeoman	VETERINARY MEDICINE
Miriam Young	WAGONS
David Webster	WITCHCRAFT—FICTION
Paul Villiard	ZOOS
Edward Ormondroyd	TROLLS
Jean Fritz	UNIVERSE
	SASQUATCH

Titles

Abominable Swamp Man	Magic Finger
Bear's Nature Guide	Navajo Slave
Black Mask Trick	Old Fashioned Girl
Cavalcade of Dragons	Paddle to the Sea
Cricket in Times Square	Quesada of Columbia
Deenie	Rabbit Finds a Way
Escape to Witch Mountain	Santa Claus Mystery
First Book of World War II	Tales from Near and Far
Freckle Juice	Tall Man from Boston
Gentle Ben	Upstairs Room
Habits of Rabbits	Valentine Cat
I Know You Al	Warrior Goddess Athena
Jasmine	Year without Santa Claus
Kermit the Hermit	Zoo Was My World
Lands End	Zia

3) 13 3x4" posterboard cards with X printed on one side and directions on the other side. For example:

Go ahead 2 spaces (2 cards)	Lose 1 turn (2 cards)
Go back 4 spaces	Take an extra turn (2 cards)
Go back to start (2 cards)	Go back 3 spaces
Go ahead 1 space	Go back 5 spaces
Go straight to finish	

4) One marker for each player.

(Materials list continues on page 104)

5) A master list with answers, to be used as an answer sheet, for each gameboard.

6) Large manila envelope (16x20") for the materials.

PROCEDURE:
1) Players arrange themselves in alphabetical order by last name, in clockwise fashion, around the playing table. The player whose last name begins with the letter closest to the beginning of the alphabet starts first.

2) All players place markers on "start."

3) Title, author, subject cards are shuffled together and placed face down on the table near the gameboard. "X" cards are shuffled and placed face down on the chest on the gameboard.

4) The first player draws a title, author, or subject card and tells in what drawer he would look to find the information.

5) If the player is correct, he moves one-half the number of spaces indicated on that card catalog drawer and places the card at the bottom of the pile. The other players may check the answer sheet to be sure that the current player is correct.

6) If the player lands on a space marked with an "X" he must draw an "X" card and follow the directions. The card then is placed at the bottom of the pile.

7) If incorrect, the player does not move his or her marker.

8) All players take turns following the same procedure.

9) The first person to reach "finish" wins and scores two points.

■ ■ ■

"C. C. PASS"

PURPOSE: To gain skill in differentiating among author cards, title cards, and subject cards.

GRADE LEVEL: Intermediate—4th and 5th grades

TIME: 25 minutes

NUMBER: Best played with a maximum of 16 students

METHOD OF CHECKING: Media specialist

MATERIALS:
1) Brown bag, large enough to hold all the treats/prizes to be awarded.
2) Treats or prizes (number to be determined by the number on any one team).
3) Timer.
4) 45 old card catalog ["c. c."] cards; 15 in each category—author, title, and subject.
5) Large manila envelope (10x13") for the materials.

PROCEDURE:
1) Divide the students into two evenly matched teams and chose a leader for each.
2) Team leaders arrange their players in the manner they think best suited for play to form a straight line.
3) Catalog cards are placed face down on a table between the two teams.
4) A timer is set for 15 or 20 minutes.
5) The team whose leader's last name begins with the letter closest to the beginning of the alphabet starts.
6) The leader from that team draws a card, shows it to everyone, and indicates whether it is an author, title, or subject card.
7) The media specialist will indicate whether the answer is correct.

(Procedures continue on page 106)

8) If correct, the card is placed in the discard pile and the player receives the brown bag (with a treat or prize for everyone on the team in it). However, *the bag is not opened* until the end of the game.

9) If incorrect, the brown bag remains on the table by the cards and the card is placed at the bottom of the pile.

10) The leader from the other team draws a card, shows it to everyone, and tells whether it is an author, title, or subject card.

11) If correct, the bag is taken either from the other team or from the table. (If incorrect, the first team either keeps the bag or it remains on the table.)

12) This procedure continues until the timer rings.

13) The team that has the bag when the timer rings gets to share the treats or prizes. (The person who last gained the bag for the team gets to draw out of the bag first and then holds the bag as the rest of the team members draw a prize without looking.)

14) Each person who answers correctly scores a point.

■ ■ ■

LOOP-THE-LOOP

PURPOSE: To practice gaining information from card catalog cards.

GRADE LEVEL: 3rd grade through 5th grade

TIME: 25 minutes

NUMBER: Best played with a maximum of 16 students

METHOD OF CHECKING: Answer sheet

MATERIALS:
1) 4 20x14" gameboards (see illustration of gameboard on page 108), or one for every group of no more than 4 students.

2) 16 markers—4 sets of 4 markers each (one marker for each student at a board).

3) Four cloth bags to keep the sets of markers in—one per set.

4) 1 spinner.

5) 100 old card catalog cards—25 per set—with questions written on them, and a number placed in the upper left-hand corner. One question per card. Sample questions:

Who is the author of the book?

When was the book published?

What is the title of this book?

Is this card annotated? If so, what does the annotation say?

6) A master sheet with both the questions (listed by number) and the answers, to be used as an answer sheet for each game board.

7) Large manila envelope (16x20") for the materials.

PROCEDURE:
1) All players place markers on "start."

2) Shuffle catalog cards and place them face down on the table near tho gameboard.

(Procedures continue on page 109)

FINISH

LOOP-THE-LOOP

START

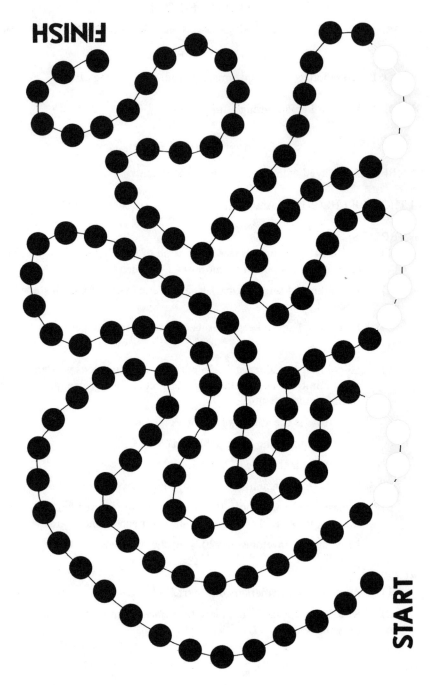

3) Players spin the spinner to determine who has the first turn, and the player who spins the highest number takes the first turn. Play goes around the table in a clockwise fashion.

4) The first player draws a catalog card from the stack and answers the question printed on it.

5) If the answer is correct, the player spins the spinner and advances that number of spaces. If incorrect, the player does not move. The other players may check the answer sheet to see if any player is correct.

6) The media specialist circulates among the tables to answer any questions that arise, and to see that game questions are being answered correctly.

7) All other players take turns, following the same procedure.

8) The winner is the first player who reaches "finish" with the exact number on the spinner to match number of circles needed to go out.

■ ■ ■

BREAK THE BANK

PURPOSE: To gain skill in locating materials by means of a subject listing.

GRADE LEVEL: Intermediate—5th and 6th grades

TIME: 25 minutes

NUMBER: Best played with a maximum of 16 students

METHOD OF CHECKING: Media specialist

MATERIALS:
1) 2 boards, with spinners and with denominations of money indicated, as shown in the illustration on page 111.

2) 312 pieces of play money in the denominations noted on the spinner board; 52 pieces per denomination.

3) 156 colored paper 3x4" cards; use one color for each denomination, 26 cards per color. Paste play money on the front of the card and write directions on the back, as in the examples shown below. Reserve the rest of the play money, to be held by the banker along with the items in number 4.

<table>
<tr><td>Find a book on:

[Subject]</td><td>$1.00</td></tr>
<tr><td>Front of card</td><td>Back of card</td></tr>
</table>

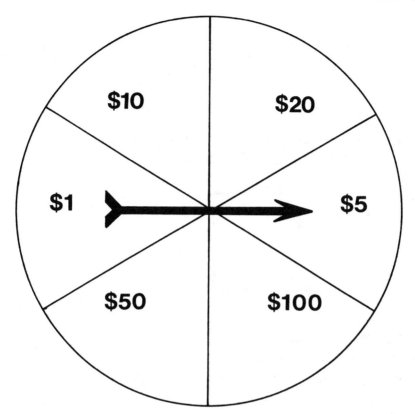

The following are suggested subjects and dollar amounts, but these can be tailored to any IMC's card catalog:

$1.00

Trees
War
Airplanes
Astronomy
Witchcraft

$5.00

Indians of North America
United States History—Revolution
Halloween
Stars
Vampires

$10.00

Fairy Tales
Dinosaurs
Pets
Holidays
Tricks

$20.00

Treasure Trove—Fiction
Religion
Birds
Poetry
Animals—Fiction

(List continues on page 112)

$50.00	$100.00
Seeds	Africa
Ships	Policemen
Trains	Snow—Fiction
Manners	Riddles
Newspaper	Fantasy

4) 30 3x4" play money cards marked "Pay to the Bearer": 5—$1.00; 5—$5.00; 5—$10.00; 5—$20.00; 5—$50.00; 5—$100.00:

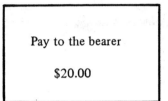

Pay to the bearer

$20.00

5) Card catalog.

6) Pencils and call slips for each player.

7) Shelf markers for each player.

8) Large manila envelope (10x13") for the materials.

PROCEDURE:

1) Play money cards are arranged on a table and a student is choosen by the media specialist to be the banker. This student acts only as the banker and does not play the game.

2) On another table, the 3x4" money/subject cards are arranged by denominations and placed between the spinners, one for each team. On one section of this table, also place the shelf markers.

3) The remaining students are divided into two evenly matched teams by counting off in twos.

4) Team members line up where the spinners are located and spin to find out from which denomination pile they should choose a subject card. (For example, if a player spins and the spinner indicates $100.00, that person is to choose a card from the $100.00 denomination pile.) When the first player has completed a spin, has drawn a subject card, and has begun to locate the material, the next team member spins. This procedure continues until all team members are simultaneously participating at different stages of play.

5) The player uses the card catalog to locate materials on the subject indicated on the money/subject cards; writes the call number, author, and title down on a slip of paper; goes to the shelf; places a shelf marker where the item belongs; and takes the item to the media specialist.

6) If the item is not on the shelf, the player shows the media specialist where the item should be located.

7) If correct, the player returns the denomination card to the banker and receives a "Pay to the Bearer" card from the banker. For example, if a player has a $1.00 denomination card, she or he receives a "Pay to the Bearer $1.00" card.

8) The player returns the material to the shelf and removes the shelf marker, places it back on the table, and cashes in the "Pay to the Bearer" card at the bank for the amount of money indicated on the card.

9) The player may then spin and begin over again.

10) The players tally their money at the end of the game, and the team with the most money wins.

■ ■ ■

WHERE ARE WE LOCATED?

PURPOSE: To practice locating books and non-print media by author, title, or subject.

GRADE LEVEL: Intermediate—4th and 5th grades

TIME: 25 minutes

NUMBER: Best played with a maximum of 16 students

METHOD OF CHECKING: Media specialist and/or answer sheet

MATERIALS:
1) A list of five fill-in-the-blank exercises on a 4x6" oak-tag and an answer sheet—made up ahead of time to coincide with each drawer in the card catalog. The answers must be kept up-to-date:

    EXAMPLE: "SM" drawer—

    Author: Solbert, Ronni
    Title:

    Author:
    Title: Small Piece of Paradise

    Author: Spier, Peter
    Title: The Erie Canal
    Publisher:
    Call Number

    Author:
    Title: A Stitch in Time
    Publisher:
    Copyright Date:
    Call Number:

(Example continues on next page)

EXAMPLE (cont'd)

> SPACE AND TIME—FICTION
> Author: Mayne, William
> Title:
> Publisher:
> Copyright Date:
> Call Number:

2) Large manila envelope (12x15") for the materials.

PROCEDURE:

1) Place the oak-tag cards with the questions on a table.

2) Have the players choose a card or give them a card.

3) Players get the card catalog drawer that matches the sheet (be certain of this) and fills in all of the information that is missing from the printed cards *on a separate piece of paper.*

4) When questions are answered, players exchange sheets with someone at their table, and compare the answers with those on the answer sheet. Or they can ask the media specialist for a new card and begin again, while the media specialist corrects the sheet(s).

5) When players are finished with a particular drawer, they are to return it to the card catalog and place it in the correct order.

6) For each item correctly answered, a player scores a point. For the example given in the materials section, the player would score 12 points if everything were answered correctly.

■ ■ ■

FOOTSTEPS

PURPOSE: To discover the types of cards that make up the card catalog and to locate the principal parts of catalog cards.

GRADE LEVEL: Intermediate—4th grade

TIME: 50 minutes

NUMBER: Best played with a maximum of 16 students

METHOD OF CHECKING: Media specialist

MATERIALS:
1) Two sets of footprints—six in each set, labeled as follows:

First footprint—author card (author's name).

Second footprint—title card (title) and call number.

Third footprint—subject card (subject) and copyright date.

Fourth footprint—"see also" card (define it).

Fifth footprint—title card (title) and whether it is fiction or non-fiction.

Sixth footprint—especially prepared card with specific author and title; must look this up in card catalog, take down call number, go to shelf and locate book, bring it back to media specialist. If the book is not on the shelf, the media specialist checks the shelf location for the book.

2) 60 old catalog cards—prepare 12 sets of 5 each, with one card each of the following types:

a) author card

b) title card

c) subject card with a copyright date

d) "see also" card

e) title card to identify whether fiction or non-fiction.

3) 12 specially prepared 3x5" cards with varying author and title, in the form below; add one of these cards to each of the above sets:

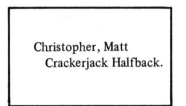

Christopher, Matt
Crackerjack Halfback.

4) Large manila envelope (12x15") for the materials.

PROCEDURE:

1) Line up two sets of footprints leading to the card catalog (six in each line).

2) Divide the class into two evenly matched teams, and appoint a leader for each team. Team leaders each receive a set of footprint cards.

3) Each student is assigned a number within the line.

4) Players not in line may play a game of Scrabble® or a similar game.

5) The first member of each team will line up behind the footprints.

6) Team captains show footprint cards in order (see number 1 in materials).

7) First person steps along side a footprint with right foot and receives a card and must identify what type of card it is (author, title, subject, etc., in the order of the prints). All this time, the player is balancing on one foot. If the other foot touches the floor, the player is out.

8) Player advances to the second footprint if the first card is correctly identified and is given a new card. Now the player is balancing on the opposite foot.

9) Continue balancing on alternate feet until all footprints have been stepped beside.

10) For each card correctly identified and for correct location of the book in question, the player scores a point—seven points in all.

11) A player who misses a card does not advance to the next footprint but goes to the end of the line, having scored points for however many cards correctly identified to that point.

(Procedures continue on page 118)

12) As soon as one player on each team is finished at the card catalog, a new player starts through the process. When the book is brought to the media specialist or the media specialist is shown where it should be located on the shelf, the player takes the place of the next person at the Scrabble® table. Also, the player that misses a card goes to the Scrabble® table and the next player comes to the footprints.

■ ■ ■

LONESOME AUTHOR

PURPOSE: To familiarize students with authors and their works.

GRADE LEVEL: Intermediate—4th and 5th grades

TIME: Part I—25 minutes
           Part II—50 minutes

NUMBER: Best played with a maximum of 16 students

METHOD OF CHECKING: Media specialist

MATERIALS:
1)   1 ditto sheet with 25 titles for each student.

2)   25 3x5" colored posterboard title cards

3)   25 3x5" colored posterboard author cards, marked as below:

```
┌─────────────────────────┐    ┌─────────────────────────┐
│ AUTHOR:                 │    │ TITLE:                  │
│                         │    │                         │
│ REY, MARGARET           │    │ CURIOUS GEORGE . . .    │
│                         │    │                         │
│                ЯOHTUA   │    │                  ƎⱢTIT   │
└─────────────────────────┘    └─────────────────────────┘
```

Titles	Authors
Curious George . . .	Rey, Margaret
Little House on the Prairie	Wilder, Laura
The Hobbit	Tolkien, J. R. R.
The Boxcar Children	Warner, Gertrude
Black Beauty	Sewell, Anna
Cat in the Hat	Dr. Seuss
Indian Festivals	Showers, Paul
The Grey King	Cooper, Susan
The Black Cauldron	Alexander, Lloyd
Where the Wild Things Are	Sendak, Maurice

(Lists continue on page 120)

Titles (cont'd)	Authors (cont'd)
Paddington Abroad	Bond, Michael
Wheel on the School	De Jong, Meindert
Magic or Not	Eager, Edward
Black Stallion	Farley, Walter
Girl Called Al	Greene, Constance
Born to Trot	Henry, Marguerite
Night Rider	Ingram, Tom
Smoky	James, Will
Gammage Cup	Kendall, Carol
Ben and Me	Lawson, Robert
Homer Price	McCloskey, Robert
Red Hart Magic	Norton, Andre
All in Good Time	Ormondroyd, Edward
Phantom Reindeer	Price, Olive
Black and Blue Magic	Snyder, Zilpha

4) Large manila envelope (10x13") for the materials.

PROCEDURE:

Part I

1) Each student is given a list of 25 titles and must find the author's name for each title.

2) Students may work in pairs and exchange answers.

3) Students are to study the completed list in preparation for PART II.

Part II

1) Students count off and divide into groups of four.

2) A group circles a table in alphabetical order by last name.

3) The player with the last name closest to the beginning of the alphabet is the dealer.

4) Dealer shuffles the cards and places three cards face down in the center of the table forming a "kitty."

5) Dealer places all other cards face down in front of each player until all cards are dealt.

6) Players pick up cards and place matching pairs of author and title cards face up on the table.

7) Players take turns drawing a card from the hand of the player on their left. Each time a pair is made, it is placed on the table.

8) A player may choose to take a card from the kitty instead of the neighbor, providing that the card is replaced with one from his hand. When all cards in the players' hands are used up except those matching the ones in the kitty, students holding the remaining cards may then choose from the kitty and exchange among themselves until all pairs are matched.

9) Dealer begins, and play moves clockwise around the table.

10) The first person to match all cards is the winner.

11) For each pair correctly matched, player receives two points. The first person "out" receives an additional three points if all pairs are correctly matched. (Optional: students may use ditto sheets from Part I.)

12) At the end of the game, the media specialist walks around to see that each pair is correctly matched.

■ ■ ■

CARD CATALOG CAPERS

PURPOSE: To answer all questions correctly, showing evidence that students know how to locate material in the card catalog.

GRADE LEVEL: Intermediate—5th and 6th grades

TIME: 50 minutes

NUMBER: Best played with a maximum of 16 students

METHOD OF CHECKING: Answer sheet

MATERIALS:
1) A list of 10 questions on a 6x9" oak-tag card and an answer sheet to coincide with each drawer in the card catalog.

   EXAMPLE: "V-Z" drawer—

   > Marguerite Vance is the author of *Windows for Rosemary*. The bottom portion of the card tells you to look in other places (tracings); name them.
   >
   > What is the call number for *Why the Chimes Rang*?
   >
   > How many books do we have with the subject heading WITCHCRAFT—FICTION?
   >
   > How many subject guides are there in the drawer? Name them.
   >
   > Under the subject heading of WEATHER is a book written by Victor C. Smith. The topic is listed only on certain pages within the book. Give the book's title and the pages for weather.
   >
   > In the drawer you will find cards with various color codings. List the color(s) and tell what type of media is indicated by it.
   >
   > Find the subject card WILDCATS—it shows the instruction "see"—. Under what subject heading should you look for WILDCATS?
   >
   > *All about Archaeology* was written by Anne White. What is the call number of the book?

What is the title of a book with the subject heading WINTER—
FICTION?

Margaret W. Brown is the author of *Wait Till the Moon Is
Full.* The card is annotated; what does the annotation say?

2) Large manila envelope (12x15") for the materials.

PROCEDURE:

1) Place the 6x9" oak-tag question cards face down on the table around
which players have gathered.

2) Have each player choose a card.

3) Students get the card catalog drawer that matches the card, and
answer all questions on paper, using that drawer as the source for
answers.

4) When the questions are answered, exchange cards with another player
at the table, and compare answers with those on the answer sheet.
Or ask the media specialist for a new card and begin again (media
specialist to correct the answers).

5) When each player is finished with a particular drawer, it is returned to
the card catalog and is placed in the correct order.

■ ■ ■

CARD CATALOG SEARCH

PURPOSE: To give students an opportunity to utilize the card catalog to locate both books and non-print media.

GRADE LEVEL: 3rd grade through 5th grade

TIME: 30 minutes

NUMBER: Best played with a maximum of 16 students.

METHOD OF CHECKING: Media specialist

MATERIALS:
1) 40 3x4" cards.
2) Prepare ahead of time clues (instructions) on the cards, such as:

Find the book *Arizona*

Find a book about KNIGHTS.

Find a book written by Ronald Syme.

Find the book *Daring Detectives*.

Find the sound filmstrip *Sounder*.

Find a book about CHEMISTRY.

Find a book about KITES.

Find *The Easy Book of Multiplication*.

Find a book written by Robert Kraus.

Find a book about DOGS—FICTION.

Find a book about FROGS.

Find the book *The Pro Quarterbacks*.

Find a book written by Tina Lee.

Find a book about BIRDS—FICTION.

Find the book *Stuart Little*.

Find the book *America Is Born*.

Find a MYSTERY AND DETECTIVE STORY.

Find transparencies about MUSIC.

Find the book *Science in Your Own Backyard*.

Find the book *Boys Life of John F. Kennedy*.

Find the book *The Real Book of Submarines*.

Find a film loop about INSECTS.

Find a book about CATS—FICTION.

Find a book about AIRPLANES.

Find a book written by Beverly Cleary.

Find a filmstrip about GHOSTS.

Find a book written by Samuel Epstein.

Find a JOKE BOOK.

Find the book *Red Fairy Book*.

Find a book with the subject heading COOKERY.

Find a filmstrip about CHRISTMAS.

Find a book about BEARS—FICTION.

Find the book *Little Town on the Prairie*.

Find a book about MARS.

Find a book written by William O. Steele.

Find the book *Caddie Woodlawn*.

Find the book *All about the Desert*.

Find the book *Famous Pioneers*.

Find a book about ELEPHANTS.

Find the book *Black Fairy Tales*.

Find a set of study prints called *Children of Other Lands*.

3) Card catalog drawers.

4) Call slips and pencils for each player.

5) Shelf markers for each player.

6) Large manila envelope (10x13") for the materials.

PROCEDURE:

1) Before the students arrive, arrange the card catalog drawers around the room, with call slips and pencils beside them.

2) Divide the players into two evenly matched teams.

(Procedures continue on page 126)

3) Place two cards for each team member on the tables around which team members are gathered.

4) Each team member takes two clue cards and hunts around the IMC for the appropriate card catalog drawer in which to look up the answers.

5) Once an item has been found, the player is to write its call number on the call slip.

6) Using the call number, each player locates the item on the shelf, takes it off of the shelf, and inserts a shelf marker in its place.

7) The player returns to the media specialist and/or aide with the item and tells whether the clue card was a title, author, or subject card, and whether the item is fiction or non-fiction.

8) If materials are not on the shelf, the media specialist checks this with the player, and if the player is correct, he or she scores a point.

9) The player who has finished two clue cards returns the items to the shelves and then helps another person on the team.

10) For each book and non-print item correctly reshelved, each player receives one point.

11) At the end of the game, each player returns a card catalog drawer to the appropriate place in the card catalog.

12) The team with the highest number of points wins.

■ ■ ■

SOLVE THE MYSTERY. . . .

PURPOSE: To demonstrate the ability to locate information in the card catalog by author, title, or subject.

GRADE LEVEL: Intermediate—5th and 6th grades

TIME: 25 minutes

NUMBER: Best played with a maximum of 16 students

METHOD OF CHECKING: Media specialist

MATERIALS:
1) Two sets of 3x5" index cards with questions on them—25 cards per set.

2) Prepare question cards such as:

   SOLVE THE MYSTERY: Find the book *The Last Battle*.

   SOLVE THE MYSTERY: Find any book in the IMC by Ruth Manning-Sanders.

   SOLVE THE MYSTERY: Find any filmstrip in the IMC about FANTASY.

3) Call slips and pencils for each student.

4) Large manila envelope (10x13") for the materials.

PROCEDURE:

Form A

1) Tell the players they are going to be media detectives, and ask them how detectives solve mysteries. (They need clues and evidence.)

2) Elicit from them the clues needed to find materials—card catalog, drawer or tray labels, guide cards, a particular catalog card. The evidence needed will be the call number, the author, and the title of the materials. Following this evidence, the mystery is solved when the materials are located on the shelf.

(Procedures continue on page 128)

3) Divide the players into two evenly matched teams, and chose a leader for each.

4) Place the cards face down in two piles on top of the card catalog, along with call slips and pencils.

5) Teams line up behind their leaders, who are standing in front of the card catalog.

6) Team leaders choose a card and locate the information required in the card catalog.

7) When the information is found, the player writes the call number on a call slip, goes to the shelves, and brings the materials to the media specialist.

8) No help is to be given by team members to one another.

9) When materials are given to the media specialist, the next person in line takes a turn. (Play this somewhat like a relay race.)

10) Each player who completes the search successfully scores a point.

11) The team that finishes first wins.

Form B

1) Same as Steps 1, 2, and 3 in Form A.

2) Arrange card catalog drawers around the room with call slips and pencils beside them.

3) Give players mystery cards that can be solved by using the card catalog drawer at a table. The media specialist passes out two mystery cards to each student.

4) Players bring the evidence, once found, to the media specialist.

5) The team finishing first wins.

■ ■ ■

"C. C. EXPLORATION"

PURPOSE: To demonstrate the ability to locate information in the card catalog by subject, then to locate an item under that subject.

GRADE LEVEL: Intermediate—6th grade

TIME: 50 minutes

NUMBER: Best played with a maximum of 16 students

METHOD OF CHECKING: Media specialist

MATERIALS:
1) Newspaper clippings (articles and pictures) representing as varied a field of subjects as possible.

2) Colored paper of all sizes and shapes. Dry-mount the newspaper items to the colored paper, then laminate; these are "C. C. Exploration" cards.

3) Call slips and pencils for each student.

4) Large manila envelope (16x20") for the materials.

PROCEDURE:
1) Divide the students into evenly matched teams, and choose a leader for each.

2) Place an equal number of "C. C. Exploration" cards on each table around which team members are gathered.

3) Members of the teams discuss under what subject they are to look in the card catalog for the topic of each "C. C. Exploration" card.

4) Once the subjects have been determined and a list made, team members line up at the card catalog, behind respective team leaders. Leaders should keep the list of subjects, so that players may refer to it when it becomes their turn.

5) Players locate the necessary information in the card catalog; write on call slips the author, title, and call number of an item on that topic, go and locate the item; and bring it back to the media specialist.

(Procedures continue on page 130)

6) When the first person's item is given to the media specialist, the next person repeats the procedure until all team members have finished.

7) Then start over, so that each player has at least two turns to look for the information.

■ ■ ■

PART III

MELVIL DEWEY'S LEGACY:
The Dewey Decimal System

    The Dewey Decimal Classification System is a method of arranging books and other materials in the IMC/library by a combination of numbers and letters. The books are classified by dividing them into ten main subject groups, which are each further broken down into more specialized fields and sub-fields. This is made possible by using a decimal point after the first three numbers. To a student coming in contact with the Dewey system for the first time, this seems rather confusing, and they continually ask, "Why can't they be filed by the author's name rather than all those numbers?" Once students understand the purpose behind the numbers, however, decimals and letters make it easy for them to find books.

    The following AV software makes it easier to explain and discuss the pros and cons of the Dewey Decimal System:

1) "The Dewey Decimal Dragon" (*Adventures in Library Land*; Educational Enrichment Materials; sound filmstrip; 10 minutes; color).

2) "The Dewey Decimal System" (*Your Library and Media Center: How to Get the Most from Them*; The Center for Humanities, Inc.; sound filmstrip; 13 minutes; color).

3) "Explaining the Dewey Decimal Classification" (*Library Services*; Eye Gate House; filmstrip; color).

4) "The Dewey Decimal System of Classification" (*Using the Library*; transparencies; black and white).

5) "The Arrangement of Books in a Library" (*How to Use the Library*; Educational Progress Corporation; audio cassette; Tape 2; 20 minutes).

6) "The Dewey Decimal System" (*How to Use the Library*; Educational Progress Corporation; audio cassette; Tape 3; 20 minutes).

PURPOSE: To locate non-fiction books on the shelves within a certain classification and to match like Dewey numbers.

GRADE LEVEL: Intermediate—5th and 6th grades

TIME: Form A—45 minutes
Form B—25 minutes

NUMBER: Best played with a maximum of 16 students

METHOD OF CHECKING: Self-checking (Form A); media specialist (Form B)

MATERIALS:
1) 100 3x4" colored posterboard cards. Place a Dewey number and its classification on pairs of cards (different numbers for each pair). Create two 50-card sets (25 pairs in each set).

HISTORY 914.4 ʎᴚOꞱSIH	TECHNOLOGY 636 ʎ⅁OꞀONHƆⱻꞱ

```
┌─────────────────────────┐   ┌─────────────────────────┐
│                         │   │                         │
│   SOCIOLOGY             │   │   LITERATURE            │
│                         │   │                         │
│                         │   │                         │
│        398.22           │   │        821              │
│                         │   │                         │
│                         │   │                         │
│       ΛƆOˡOIƆOS          │   │      Ǝꓤ∩⊥∀ꓤƎ⊥Iˡ          │
│                         │   │                         │
└─────────────────────────┘   └─────────────────────────┘
```

2) 16 strips of colored posterboard to be used as markers.

3) Large manila envelope (9x12") for the materials.

4) Form B requires shelf markers.

PROCEDURE:

Form A

1) Four to eight players gather around each set of tables or in a circle on the floor in alphabetical order.

2) Student with the last name closest to the beginning of the alphabet is the dealer.

3) Dealer shuffles cards and places them face down on the table or floor. The cards may be laid out in any pattern, but no two cards should touch each other.

4) Each player will want to remember the position of each card as it is turned up on the table or floor, since this will help in building pairs.

5) The dealer starts the game by turning face up any two cards, one at a time. All players look at the two cards as they are turned up, but the two cards are not immediately picked up, just turned face up.

6) If the two cards are a pair, the dealer picks them up, keeps them, and turns up two more cards. The dealer's turn continues as long as each two cards turned up are a pair. A pair consists of the same classification and the same number (for example, History—917.4).

7) If the two cards are not a pair, they are turned face down again and left in their original places. This ends the dealer's turn. (Cards are picked up *only* when they are a pair.)

(Procedures continue on page 134)

8) After the dealer's turn is over, the player to the left of the dealer continues the game. Play continues around the table or circle on the floor to the left, as above.

9) The winner is the player who has accumulated the greatest number of pairs after all of the cards have been picked up from the table or floor.

10) Each player scores one point for each pair held by that person at the end of the game.

Form B

1) Each player records, on paper, the pairs that she or he has matched in Form A and goes to the shelves to find the books bearing those Dewey numbers.

2) When each book is found, a shelf marker is inserted in the space. The book is brought to the media specialist for checking, then returned to the shelves. If a book cannot be found, the student is to show the media specialist where it belongs on the shelves.

3) For each book found and reshelved correctly, the student scores two points. Shelf markers are left in place so that the media specialist may check to see if the book is reshelved correctly.

■ ■ ■

PURPOSE: To facilitate the teaching and learning of the main classifications of the Dewey Decimal Classification System.

GRADE LEVEL: Intermediate—5th and 6th grades

TIME: 15-20 minutes each round

NUMBER: Best played with a maximum of 16 students

METHOD OF CHECKING: Media specialist

MATERIALS:
1)   1 10x12" colored posterboard call sheet for the media specialist, marked as below:

CALL SHEET

D	E¹	W	E²	Y
000	000	000	000	000
100	100	100	100	100
200	200	200	200	200
300	300	300	300	300
400	400	400	400	400
500	500	500	500	500
600	600	600	600	600
700	700	700	700	700
800	800	800	800	800
900	900	900	900	900

(Materials list continues on page 136)

2)   50 2x1" colored posterboard call tokens; see illustration on page 135 for notations, and mark as below:

D—General Works	E—Sociology
(000)	(300) 1

D—Language	E—History
(400)	(900) 2

3)   20 5x6" colored posterboard Dewey Bingo Cards: each card should be numbered with different main classification numbers at random.

BINGO CARD

D	E¹	W	E²	Y
2 0 0	6 0 0	1 0 0	9 0 0	0 0 0
8 0 0	4 0 0	3 0 0	1 0 0	2 0 0
3 0 0	2 0 0	7 0 0	6 0 0	4 0 0
5 0 0	1 0 0	5 0 0	4 0 0	9 0 0
9 0 0	8 0 0	9 0 0	3 0 0	5 0 0

4)   16 "Curious George Wants to Know about the Dewey Decimal Classification System" bookmarks.

5)   500 plastic tokens, 25 each placed in a letter-sized envelope or cloth pouch.

6)   20 letter-sized envelopes or cloth pouches.

7)   Large manila envelope (16x20") for the materials.

PROCEDURE:

1) Each student is given 1 "Dewey Bingo" card, a bookmark, and an envelope with plastic tokens.

2) The media specialist places the call tokens in a box or bowl to use in drawing classifications to call out.

3) The media specialist draws one call token, reads the letter and subject heading printed on it (for example, "Y—Literature"). Note: the Dewey number that appears in the parentheses on each call token is for the media specialist's reference only and should not be called.

4) Each player looks at the appropriate row on her or his "Dewey Bingo" card (in this case, the row below "Y"). If the correct Dewey number for the subject heading that is called (in the example, 800) appears in that row on the player's card, the player covers it with a plastic token.

5) The media specialist places the call token in the corresponding space on the call sheet, draws another, and calls it out as before.

6) Play continues in this manner until a player covers 5 correct numbers in a row—vertically, horizontally, or diagonally—and calls "Dewey" to indicate winning.

7) For accuracy's sake, the winner should read off the numbers covered so that the media specialist can check them against the numbers for the subject headings that have been called.

8) The winning player in each instance is to receive a certain number of points—to be determined by the media specialist.

9) Variations of the game include:

a) Four Corners—All four corners must be covered with tokens to win.

b) Picture Frame—All squares on the outside of the card must be covered with tokens to win.

c) Black-Out—All squares must be covered with tokens to win.

■ ■ ■

PURPOSE: To acquaint students with the ten main classifications of the Dewey Decimal Classification System.

GRADE LEVEL: Intermediate—4th grade

TIME: 25 minutes

NUMBER: Best played with a maximum of 16 students

METHOD OF CHECKING: Answer sheet

MATERIALS:
1)   8 9x12" tag-board "High Flyers" gameboards, as shown on page 139.

2)   80 2x3" colored posterboard cards bearing a Dewey main classification heading (for a total of 8 10-card sets). On the back of the cards, indicate the number of the set (1-8).

3)   80 2x3" colored posterboard cards bearing a Dewey number (for a total of 8 10-card sets). On the back of the cards, indicate the number of the set (1-8).

```
┌─────────────────────────┐
│                         │
│                         │
│                         │
│           200           │
│                         │
│                         │
└─────────────────────────┘
```

(Materials list continues on page 140)

HIGH FLYERS

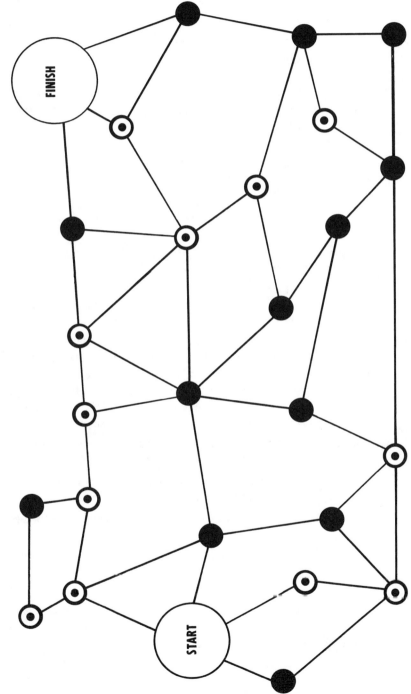

4)   16 markers (one for each student).

5)   8 small discs (one side red, the other side green).

6)   2 master sheets with answers corresponding to the cards.

7)   Large manila envelope (12x15") for the materials.

PROCEDURE:

1)   Divide the students into pairs, and give each pair of students a "High Flyers" card, a marker, and 2 sets of cards (one classification set and one number set).

2)   Appoint two players as team leaders; they are each responsible for the correct answers of 8 players. During play, they are to walk around with master sheets of answers and constantly check.

3)   The player with the last name closest to the beginning of the alphabet goes first.

4)   Each pair of players places the shuffled cards (20) face down on the playing area in a stack.

5)   The first player picks up a card and, if it has a Dewey classification, asks the partner to give the Dewey number; or, if it has a Dewey number, the player must give the Dewey classification.

6)   If correct, the answering player tosses a small disc (solid color on one side, circle with a dot on the other side). If the disc lands with the solid colored circle up, the player can move his or her marker only to a solid circle on the gameboard; if it lands with the dotted circle up, the player moves only to a dotted circle on the gameboard. If the player is blocked and cannot move to that color, she or he remains and waits another turn.

7)   If incorrect, the player loses that turn to move, and the other player is shown a card from which to identify the required information.

8)   Each player is to keep track on a small slip of paper of the number personally answered correctly. Each correct answer counts as one point.

9)   The first person to reach finish adds two points to that score for a final score.

■   ■   ■

BOOK TITLE BINGO

PURPOSE: To become proficient at identifying where non-fiction book titles fall within the Dewey Decimal Classification System.

GRADE LEVEL: Intermediate—6th grade

TIME: 25 minutes per round

NUMBER: Best played with a maximum of 16 students

METHOD OF CHECKING: Media specialist

MATERIALS:
  1) 1 10x12" colored posterboard call sheet for the media specialist. See "Dewey Bingo," page 135, for board form, substituting $T^1 I T^2 L E$ for $D E^1 W E^2 Y$.

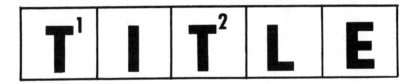

  2) 50 2x1" colored posterboard call tokens (shown on page 143) (5 for each main classification) with titles printed one to a card and taken from each classification, as below:

Dewey Classification 000	Dewey Classification 100
Complete Book of Marvels	Ghosts and Witches Aplenty
The Greatest Monsters in the World	Tall Man from Boston
Unidentified Flying Objects	Sixth Sense
The Trivia Encyclopedia	I Was So Mad!
On the Track of Bigfoot	Goops and How to Be Them

(Materials list continues on page 142)

Dewey Classification 200	Dewey Classification 300
In the Beginning: Stories from the Bible Story of Persephone God Is in the Mountain Golden God: Apollo Hanukkah	First Book of American Negroes Nature Sleuths: Protectors of Our Wildlife Exploring under the Sea Magic Calabash: Folk Tales from America's Islands and Alaska Squirrel's Song: A Hopi Indian Tale
Dewey Classification 400	Dewey Classification 500
My First Book of Words: Their Family Histories Word Origins and Their Romantic Stories Tree of Language French Alphabet and Numbers for Children American Heritage Dictionary	Mr. Wizard's Science Secrets Biography of a Caribou Hurricanes and Twisters Who's in the Egg? Sharks
Dewey Classification 600	Dewey Classification 700
Story of Your Bones Experiments in Optical Illusion All about Radio and Television Horse Called Dragon From Trees to Paper: The Story of Newsprint	Art of the North American Indian Great Houses of American History African Crafts for You to Make Book of Tricks and Magic Great American Book of Sidewalk Games
Dewey Classification 800	Dewey Classification 900
Witch Poems Christmas Tree Haiku: The Mood of the Earth Quangle Wangle's Hat Just for Fun: Humorous Stories and Poems	All about Archaeology Colorado Story of the Sioux Doctors in Petticoats To California by Covered Wagon

Call Tokens

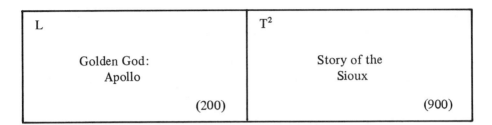

L	T²
Golden God: Apollo	Story of the Sioux
(200)	(900)

3) 20 5x6" colored posterboard "Title" bingo cards. See "Dewey Bingo," page 136, for form, substituting T^1 I T^2 L E for D E^1 W E^2 Y.

4) 500 plastic tokens, 25 each placed in a letter-sized envelope or cloth pouch.

5) 20 letter-sized envelopes or cloth pouches for the tokens.

6) Large manila envelope (16x20") for the materials.

PROCEDURE:

1) Each player is given 1 book title bingo card and an envelope or pouch of plastic tokens.

2) The media specialist places the printed call tokens in a box or bowl to use in drawing titles to call out.

3) The media specialist draws one call token and reads the letter and book title printed on it (for example, "L–*Book of Tricks and Magic*").

4) Each player looks at the appropriate row on the "Book Title Bingo" card (in this case, the row below L). If the correct Dewey number for the book title called (in the example, 700) appears in that row on the player's card, the player covers it with a plastic token.

(Procedures continue on page 144)

5) The media specialist places the call token in the corresponding space on the call sheet, draws another, and calls it out as before.

6) Play continues in this manner until a player covers 5 correct numbers in a row—vertically, horizontally, or diagonally—and calls "Title" to indicate winning.

7) For accuracy's sake, the player should read off the numbers covered so the media specialist can check them against the numbers for the titles that have been called.

8) The winning player in each instance is to receive a certain number of points—to be determined by the media specialist.

9) Variations of the game include:

    a) Four Corners—All four corners must be covered with tokens to win.

    b) Picture Frame—All squares on the outside of the card must be covered with tokens to win.

    c) Black-Out—All squares must be covered with tokens to win.

■ ■ ■

$\diamond\!\!\!\diamond\!\!\!\diamond\!\!\!\diamond\!\!\!\diamond\!\!\!\diamond\!\!\!\diamond\!\!\!\diamond\!\!\!\diamond\!\!\!\diamond\!\!\!\diamond\!\!\!\diamond\!\!\!\diamond\!\!\!\diamond\!\!\!\diamond\!\!\!\diamond$

I DOUBT IT!!!

$\diamond\!\!\!\diamond\!\!\!\diamond\!\!\!\diamond\!\!\!\diamond\!\!\!\diamond\!\!\!\diamond\!\!\!\diamond\!\!\!\diamond\!\!\!\diamond\!\!\!\diamond\!\!\!\diamond\!\!\!\diamond\!\!\!\diamond\!\!\!\diamond\!\!\!\diamond\!\!\!\diamond$

PURPOSE: To acquaint students with the ten main classifications of the Dewey Decimal Classification System.

GRADE LEVEL: Intermediate—4th grade through 6th grade

TIME: 45 minutes

NUMBER: Best played with a maximum of 16 students

METHOD OF CHECKING: Self-checking

MATERIALS:
1)   150 3x4" colored posterboard cards bearing a classification number (50 cards to each of three sets; 5 cards each within each set for the ten main classifications).

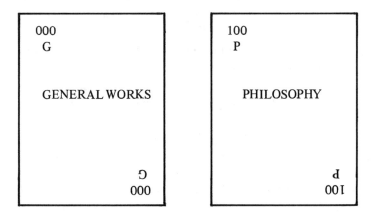

2)   Large manila envelope (10x13") for the materials.

PROCEDURE:
1)   Three to six students gather around a set of tables or in a circle on the floor in alphabetical order.

(Procedures continue on page 146)

2) Student with the last name closest to the beginning of the alphabet is the dealer.

3) Dealer shuffles and deals out all of the cards—one at a time from left to right. It does not matter if some players get an extra card on the last round of the deal.

4) Players sort cards by number and classification.

5) In this game, it is fair to fool (bluff) the other players by not playing the card or cards that a player *says* she or he is playing. However, if caught playing the wrong cards, a player must pay a penalty: pick up all the cards on the table. (And the object here is to run out of cards as fast as possible.)

6) Play cards face down on the table so that no one can see them.

7) Beginning with those cards within the 000s, each player takes a turn playing from one to five cards face down on the table. (After the 000s are played once, the 100s are played, then the 200s, 300s, etc.) Each time, the player must identify the classification by saying what it is: "two 300s, Sociology."

8) Actually, a student *may play any card* but *must pretend* to be playing the card it is his or her turn to play. By trying to fool the others this way, a player tries to be the first player to run out of cards.

9) No one can play more than five cards because there are only five 000s, five 100s, and so on.

10) When laying down cards, players must announce how many cards are being played and what they are *supposed* to be ("One 900—History," or "Two 900s—History," even if they are not 900s). If one player does not believe another, he or she says, "I doubt it."

11) Anyone may say, "I doubt it," but only after a player has placed the cards face down on the table and has stated how many, what number of classification, and the classification name that they are to be (or pass as). (If two players say, "I doubt it," at the same time, the player closest to the left of the player laying down the cards is recognized as the "doubter.") When a player is doubted, all of the cards played must be picked up by the player or the "doubter," as appropriate.

12) The winner is the first player out of cards.

(A sample game appears on page 147)

SAMPLE GAME

1) The player to the left of the dealer (Player 1) begins the game.
Player 1 must begin playing 000s; Player 1 does not have a 000, but
must play a card. Player 1 decides to get rid of two cards and plays a
200 and a 500 face down on the table and says, "two 000s—General
Works." No one says, "I doubt it." Everyone believes him.

2) Player 2 to the left of Player 1 continues the game, but now must play
100s. Player 2 has two 100s, but she wants to get rid of another card,
along with the two 100s. Player 2 plays the two 100s and a 300 and
says, "three 100s—Philosophy." Player 1 says, "I doubt it," so
Player 2 has to show everyone the cards that she played. Because they
are not three 100s, Player 2 must pick up *all* of the cards on the table
that have been played.

3) Player 3 continues the game, and goes on to play the 200s. Player 3
has one 200 and says, "One 200—Religion." No one says, "I doubt
it," so the player to the left of Player 3 continues the game.

4) This is Player 4, whose turn it is to play 300s. Three 300s are put face
down on the table and Player 4 says, "Three 300s—Sociology."
Player 2 says, "I doubt it." Player 4 shows everyone the cards. Because
the cards were three 300s, Player 2, who doubted, must pick up all the
cards on the table.

5) Play continues as before, with each player taking his or her turn playing 400s, 500s, and so on, up to 900s. After the 900s are played,
the next player begins again with the 000s.

■ ■ ■

PURPOSE: To demonstrate the ability to correctly identify where subordinate subject divisions fall within classifications.

GRADE LEVEL: Intermediate—5th and 6th grades

TIME: 25 minutes per round

NUMBER: Best played with a maximum of 16 students

METHOD OF CHECKING: Media specialist

MATERIALS:
   1)   1 10x12" colored posterboard call sheet for the media specialist. See "Dewey Bingo," page 135, for board form, substituting G R O U P for D E[1] W E[2] Y.

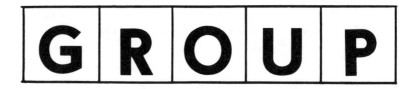

   2)   50 2x1" colored posterboard call tokens, illustrated on page 149, marked similarly to those below:

G	Unidentified Flying Objects (000)	G	Psychology (100)
R	Encyclopedias (000)	R	Witchcraft (100)
O	World Records (000)	O	Ancient Philosophers (100)
U	Bibliographies (000)	U	Modern Philosophers (100)
P	Library Science (000)	P	Astrology (100)
G	Bible Stories (200)	G	Law (300)
R	Mythology (200)	R	Education (300)
O	Religious History (200)	O	Folklore (300)
U	Devotions and Prayers (200)	U	Politics (300)
P	The Bible (200)	P	Minorities (300)

G	English Grammar (400)	G	Mathematics (500)
R	Italian Dictionaries (400)	R	Chemistry (500)
O	French Grammar (400)	O	Biology (500)
U	German Dictionaries (400)	U	Astronomy (500)
P	Dictionaries of Synonyms (400)	P	Geology (500)
G	Codes (600)	G	Drawing (700)
R	Space Exploration (600)	R	Music (700)
O	Aviation (600)	O	Photography (700)
U	Medicine (600)	U	Sculpture (700)
P	Engineering (600)	P	Architecture (700)
G	American Literature (800)	G	Geography (900)
R	Spanish Poetry (800)	R	American Indians (900)
O	French Literature (800)	O	Collective Biography (900)
U	Greek Literature (800)	U	Travel (900)
P	English Poetry (800)	P	American History (900)

Call Token

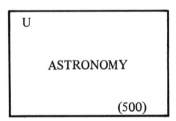

3) 20 5x6" colored posterboard "Group" bingo cards. See "Dewey
    Bingo," page 136, for form, substituting G R O U P for
    D E[1] W E[2] Y.

(Materials list continues on page 150)

4) 500 plastic tokens with 25 each placed in a small envelope or cloth pouch.

5) 20 letter-sized envelopes or cloth pouches for the tokens.

6) Large manila envelope (16x20") for the materials.

PROCEDURE:

1) Each player is given 1 "Group Bingo" card and an envelope (or pouch) of plastic tokens.

2) The media specialist places the printed call tokens in a box or bowl to use in drawing subjects to call out.

3) The media specialist draws one call token and reads the letter and subordinate subject division printed on it (for example, "U—Travel").

4) Each player looks at the appropriate row on the "Group Bingo" card (in this case, the row below U). If the correct Dewey number for the subordinate subject division called (in the example, 900) appears in that row on the player's card, the player covers it with a plastic token.

5) The media specialist places the printed call token in the corresponding space on the call sheet, draws another, and calls it out as before.

6) Play continues in this manner until a player covers 5 correct numbers in a row—vertically, horizontally, or diagonally—and calls "Group" to indicate winning.

7) For accuracy's sake, the player should read off the numbers covered so that the media specialist can check them against the numbers for the subject headings that have been called.

8) The winning player in each instance is to receive a certain number of points—to be determined by the media specialist.

9) Variations of the game include:

   a) Four Corners—All four corners must be covered with tokens to win.

   b) Picture Frame—All squares on the outside of the card must be covered with tokens to win.

   c) Black-Out—All squares must be covered with tokens to win.

■ ■ ■

DEWEY BASKETBALL

PURPOSE: To familiarize students with the ten main Dewey classifications and the subjects to be found within each classification.

GRADE LEVEL: Intermediate—5th grade

TIME: 25 minutes

NUMBER: Best played with a maximum of 16 students

METHOD OF CHECKING: Media specialist

MATERIALS:
1) 1 wastepaper basket.

2) 2 erasers or balls.

3) A coin of any denomination.

4) Master list of the ten classifications and the subjects within each; dry-mounted to a piece of colored posterboard. (See "Name That Answer," page 156, for a listing of classifications and subjects.)

5) 1 student will be needed to keep score.

6) Large manila envelope (10x13") for the master list.

PROCEDURE:
1) Divide the students into two evenly matched teams, and choose a leader for each.

2) The teams are to stand in straight lines—one team on each side of the room.

3) Between the teams, at an equal distance from each, is placed the wastepaper basket.

4) The team leader whose last name is closest to the beginning of the alphabet is first to call "heads" or "tails" and flips the coin. Whichever team's leader calls the flip correctly is first.

5) Give each leader an eraser to use tor that team.

6) The player who is first in line on the starting team takes the eraser and throws it at the basket.

(Procedures continue on page 152)

7) If a basket is made, the media specialist reads a classification and number (e.g., 000—General Works) and the player must give a subject (e.g., Bigfoot—Sasquatch).

8) If the player is correct, that person scores two points (one for the basket and one for the correct answer), and play switches to the second team.

9) If incorrectly identified, no points are awarded and the first player on the opposing team gets a chance to answer for two points. If correct, that player then takes his or her own turn as well, following the procedure in item 6. If that player is incorrect, play goes back to the first team (second player begins).

10) When a basket is not made, the player still receives one point for correctly identifying a subject within a classification and number.

11) A player who is finished goes to the end of the line and awaits another turn.

12) Throughout the game, the student appointed scorekeeper will be keeping the scores for individual players. At the end of a team's turn, the scorekeeper will be given a chance to score his or her own points.

13) Scoring is the same for the entire game.

14) The team whose members have the most points combined at the end of the game is declared winner and given a certain number of extra points—to be determined by the media specialist.

■ ■ ■

DING BAT

PURPOSE: To familiarize students with the ten main Dewey classifications and the subjects to be found within each classification.

GRADE LEVEL: Intermediate—6th grade

TIME: 25 minutes

NUMBER: Best played with a maximum of 16 students

METHOD OF CHECKING: Media specialist

MATERIALS:
1)   a.   120 3x4" colored posterboard classification cards (30 cards forming a set—4 sets). Use each of the ten classifications three times, and mark as below.

      b.   120 3x4" colored posterboard subject cards (30 cards forming a set—4 sets). For each classification, use three different subjects, and mark as below.

      c.   4 3x4" "odd cards" ("Ding Bat")—one for each deck.

      d.   Thus, each deck should contain 30 classification cards (with each classification used three times), 30 subject cards (three subject cards per classification), and 1 "Ding Bat" card, for a total of 61 cards per deck. Label each deck (1, 2, 3, or 4) on the back of every card in it.

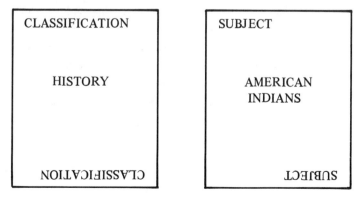

(Materials list continues on page 154)

2)   Master list of the ten main classifications and the subjects within each; dry-mounted to a piece of colored posterboard. (See "Name That Answer," page 156, for a listing of classifications and subjects.)

3)   Large manila envelope (10x13") for the materials.

PROCEDURE:

1)   3-4 students gather around a table in alphabetical order by last name.

2)   The student with the last name closest to the beginning of the alphabet is the dealer.

3)   Dealer shuffles the cards from one set and distributes them one at a time until the pack is exhausted. If every player does not receive the same number of cards, it does not matter.

4)   Players match pairs (CLASSIFICATION–Science is *matched with* SUBJECT–Stars) and place these cards face down in front of them, without showing them to the other players.

5)   All of the cards laid out in this manner are to be left in front of the player, in order to discover errors, if any.

6)   The discarding of pairs complete, the dealer begins by spreading her or his remaining cards, like a fan, without showing them to other players; the dealer then presents the back of the "fan" to the left-hand neighbor, who must draw one card at random.

7)   The card drawn is examined, and if it completes a pair, the two cards are discarded.

8)   Whether the card drawn forms a pair or not, that player's cards are then spread and presented (back of fan) to the next player on the left, to be drawn from in the same manner. (Of course, any pair formed in this way would be placed with that player's other pairs.)

9)   This process of drawing, forming pairs, and discarding is continued until one player remains with one card.

10)   This card is, of course, the "Ding Bat" card, and the unfortunate holder of it is the "Ding Bat," but only for that deal.

11)   When all cards are laid out and turned over, the media specialist is to walk around and check to see if all cards are correctly matched.

12)   For each pair correctly matched, a player scores two points.

■   ■   ■

PURPOSE: To acquaint students with the ten main classifications of the Dewey Decimal Classification System and the subjects to be found within each classification.

GRADE LEVEL: Intermediate—5th grade

TIME: 25 minutes

NUMBER: Best played with a maximum of 16 students

METHOD OF CHECKING: Media specialist

MATERIALS:
1) Ten 8x10" colored posterboard cards, each labeled with one of these divisions and titles:

000-099	General Works
100-199	Philosophy—Who Am I?
200-299	Religion—Who Made Me?
300-399	Sociology—Who Is the Man in the Next Cave?
400-499	Languages—How Can I Make That Man Understand Me?
500-599	Science—What Makes Things Happen in the World around Me?
600-699	Applied Science or Technology—How Can I Control Nature?
700-799	Arts and Recreation—How Can I Enjoy My Spare Time?
800-899	Literature—What Are the Stories of Man's Great Deeds and Thoughts?
900-999	History—"How Can I Record What Man Has Done?

2) 80 3x3" colored posterboard cards (forming two 40-card sets); use two different colors—red for one set, orange for the other set. On each card, print a subject that is found within one of the broad classifications in step 1:

(Materials list continues on page 156)

Dewey Classification 000

Unidentified Flying Objects
Superstition
Library Science
Bigfoot—Sasquatch

Dewey Classification 100

Witchcraft
Astrology
Manners

Dewey Classification 200

Bible Stories
Mythology
Christmas—Nativity

Dewey Classification 300

Careers
Government
Trains
Almanacs
Diplomacy
Customs
Holidays
Folklore
Fairy Tales
Metric System

Dewey Classification 400

Dictionaries
Thesaurus
Grammar Books
Word Origins

Dewey Classification 500

Insects
Animals
Flowers
Birds
Rocks
Stars

Dewey Classification 500 (cont'd)

Planets
Math
Trees
Biology
Weather
Volcanoes
Earthquakes
Electricity
Prehistoric Times

Dewey Classification 600

Codes
Plants
Medicine
Ships
Cars
Airplanes
Pets
Space Exploration
Invention
Engineering

Dewey Classification 700

Painting
Music
Hobbies
Theater
Humor-Jokes/Riddles
Sports
Photography
Stamp Collecting
Coin Collecting
Movie Monsters
Sculpture

Dewey Classification 800

Poetry
Plays

Dewey Classification 900

Collective Biography
Geography
Wars
American Indians
Atlases
Arctic Exploration
Ancient History
Modern History

3) Dittoed lists of classifications and subjects—one for each student.

4) Master list of the ten classifications and the subjects within each; dry-mounted to a piece of colored posterboard.

5) Large manila envelope (12x15") for the materials.

PROCEDURE:

1) *In the period before this game is to be played*, give each student a dittoed list of classifications and the subjects found within each.

2) One player chosen as overall game leader is given the set of classification cards.

3) Divide the remaining students into two evenly matched teams and choose leaders for each.

4) One set of subject cards is given to each team leader, who then distributes the cards to team members. Each player should receive at least five cards.

5) The teams line up behind their leaders on one side of the room.

6) The game leader is placed at the opposite side of the room.

7) The game leader then shuffles and holds up a classification card.

8) One player from each team, who thinks he or she has the correct subject card, must walk (not run) over to the game leader and tag that person's hand.

9) Whichever player tags the game leader's hand first gets a point, if the answer is correct.

10) If correct, the subject card is left with the game leader and placed in a pile, either to the leader's left or right depending on placement of team. If incorrect, the player returns with the card to his or her team to try gain. The other team member then has a chance to place a card.

(Procedures continue on page 158)

11) The media specialist is to be beside the game leader with the master list, in case a dispute over who is right arises.

12) The team that has deposited the most subject cards with the game leader wins the match.

13) Each team leader is to keep track of the points scored by each individual on that team.

■ ■ ■

LONESOME DEWEY

PURPOSE: To familiarize students with the ten main Dewey classifications and the subjects to be found within each classification.

GRADE LEVEL: Intermediate—5th and 6th grades

TIME: Part I—25 minutes
        Part II—35-40 minutes

NUMBER: Best played with a maximum of 16 students

METHOD OF CHECKING: Media specialist

MATERIALS:
1)   Ditto sheets with the ten main classifications printed on them.

2)   a.   120 3x4" colored posterboard classification cards (30 cards, forming a set—4 sets). Use each classification three times, and mark as below.

     b.   120 3x4" colored posterboard subject cards (30 cards, forming a set—4 sets). For each classification, use three different subjects, and mark as below.

     c.   Thus, each deck should contain 30 classification cards (with each classification used three times), 30 subject cards (three subject cards per classification), for a total of 60 cards per deck. Label each deck (1, 2, 3, or 4) on the back of every card in it.

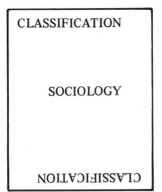

(Materials list continues on page 160)

3) Master list of the ten main classifications and the subjects within each; dry-mounted to a piece of colored posterboard. (See "Name That Answer," page 156, for a listing of classifications and subjects.)

4) Large manila envelope (10x13") for the materials.

PROCEDURE:

Part I

1) Each student is given a list of the ten classifications—they must find as many subjects as they can for each classification.

2) Students may work in pairs and exchange answers.

3) Students are to study these sheets in preparation for Part II.

Part II

1) Students count off in fours and divide into groups.

2) The player in each group with the last name closest to the beginning of the alphabet is the dealer.

3) Dealer shuffles cards and places three cards face down in the center of the table, forming a "kitty."

4) Dealer then deals all of the other cards face down in front of the players until all cards are gone.

5) Players pick up cards and place matching pairs face down on the table.

6) The dealer beginning, players take turns drawing a card from the hand of the player on their left. Each time a pair is made, it should be placed on the table.

7) A player may choose to take a card from the kitty instead of the neighbor, providing that the card is replaced with one from his hand. When all cards in the players' hands are used up except those matching the ones in the kitty, students holding the remaining cards may then choose from the kitty and exchange among themselves until all pairs are matched.

8) First person to match all cards is the winner.

9) For each pair correctly matched, the player receives two points. First person to go "out" receives an additional 3 points if all pairs are correct.

10) At the end of the game, the media specialist will check to see that each pair is correctly matched.

■ ■ ■

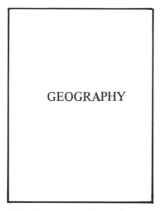

```
╲╱╲╱╲╱╲╱╲╱╲╱╲╱╲╱╲╱╲╱╲╱╲╱╲╱╲╱╲╱╲╱╲╱╲╱╲╱╲╱╲╱╲╱╲╱
```

KING OF THE CASTLE

```
╲╱╲╱╲╱╲╱╲╱╲╱╲╱╲╱╲╱╲╱╲╱╲╱╲╱╲╱╲╱╲╱╲╱╲╱╲╱╲╱╲╱╲╱╲╱
```

PURPOSE: To familiarize students with the ten main Dewey classifications and the subjects to be found within each classification.

GRADE LEVEL: Intermediate—5th and 6th grades

TIME: 50 minutes

NUMBER: Best played with a maximum of 16 students

METHOD OF CHECKING: Self-checking

MATERIALS:
1) 240 3x4" colored posterboard "Dewey Subject Cards" (30 cards to a set for a total of 8 sets). On one side of the card, print the subject ("geography"); on the reverse print the classification (900—History) and the set number in the lower right-hand corner (1-8). (See "Name That Answer," page 156, for a listing of classifications and subjects.)

GEOGRAPHY	900 HISTORY
Side facing the "king"	Side facing the "joker"

2) 8 crowns made of gold paper.
3) 8 hats made of silver paper.
4) 16 "Curious George Wants to Know about the Dewey Decimal Classification System" bookmarks.

(Materials list continues on page 162)

5) Large manila envelope (16x20") for the materials.

PROCEDURE:
1) Students are paired and the media specialist chooses a "king" and "joker" for each pair. The "king" sits on a "throne" (a chair) and wears a gold crown. The "joker" sits across from the king holding a set of "Dewey Subject Cards" and wears a silver hat.

2) For each card the joker holds up, the king must give the correct classification and number. (For example, the joker holds up "photography," the king must answer "700—Fine Arts or Arts and Recreation" to be correct.)

3) The king retains the throne until failing to give a correct classification and number. When this happens the joker becomes king.

4) Until a student becomes familiar with the subjects within the classifications, the "Curious George" bookmarks may be used.

5) The jokers keep score on a piece of paper.

6) All of the kings with a perfect score (30 correct answers) or tied scores may compete with each other until there is an overall winner.

7) All of the jokers with tied scores compete until there is a winner.

8) The winning king plays off with the winning joker.

9) The king or joker with the highest score is then declared the overall winner within the group.

■ ■ ■

FOOTBALL GRID

PURPOSE: To correctly identify a Dewey number with its classification and the corresponding subjects within each classification.

GRADE LEVEL: Intermediate—6th grade

TIME: 25 minutes

NUMBER: Best played with a maximum of 16 students

METHOD OF CHECKING: Self-checking

MATERIALS:
1) 1 Football Grid gameboard (see illustration on page 164), made from 20x14" colored posterboard.
2) 1 football made from colored posterboard.
3) a. 80 4x4" colored posterboard cards to form 2 sets, marked with 10 classifications, 10 numbers, and 20 subjects (2 for each classification) per set, for a total of 40 cards per set.
    b. The front side should have a number, classification, or subject and will be held toward the players. The back side should have:
    1) if a number on front, then a classification;
    2) if a classification on front, then a number;
    3) if a subject on front, then both a classification and number.

    Also indicate on the back (in lower right-hand corner) whether it is set 1 or 2.

    Illustrations of cards are on page 165.
4) A coin of any denomination.
5) Large manila envelope (16x20") for the materials.

(Procedures begin on page 166)

FOOTBALL GRID

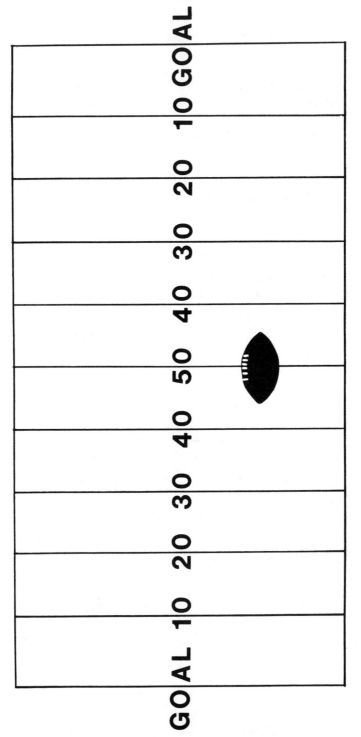

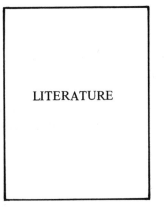

LITERATURE

Front view

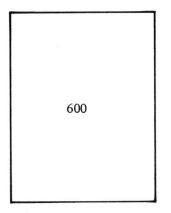

600

Front view

Earthquakes

Front view

800

1

Back view

TECHNOLOGY

2

Back view

SCIENCE
500

1

Back view

PROCEDURE:
1) Divide the students into two evenly matched teams, and choose leaders for each.

2) Each leader is given a set of cards and told how to hold them: the classification, number, or subject faces the team, and the answer side (with the set number) faces the leader.

3) The team leader whose last name is closest to the beginning of the alphabet is first to call "heads" or "tails" and flips the coin. Whichever leader calls the flip correctly begins.

4) Each leader shuffles the cards in a set.

5) The teams are to sit facing the opposing leader.

6) The first leader shows a card to members of the opposing team. If a number is on the front, a classification is required; if a classification is on the front, a number is required; if a subject is on the front, then both a number and a classification are required. Players raise hands if they know the answer.

7) For each correct answer, the football is moved 10 yards on the game-board, and the player scores three points. The media specialist will keep scores.

8) A team may score 2 touchdowns, and then the ball goes to the other team.

9) If an answer is incorrect, it is a "fumble" and the ball goes to the other team.

10) At the end of the game, the team with the greatest number of touch-downs is the winner.

■ ■ ■

DO YOU KNOW YOUR DEWEY DECIMAL CLASSIFICATION???

PURPOSE: To review the meaning of the divisions within the Dewey Decimal Classification System.

GRADE LEVEL: Intermediate—5th and 6th grades

TIME: 50 minutes

NUMBER: Best played with a maximum of 16 students

METHOD OF CHECKING: Self-checking

MATERIALS:

1) Ten 8x10" colored posterboard cards, each labeled with (only) one of these Dewey divisions and titles:

000-099	General Works
100-199	Philosophy—Who Am I?
200-299	Religion—Who Made Me?
300-399	Sociology—Who Is the Man in the Next Cave?
400-499	Languages—How Can I Make That Man Understand Me?
500-599	Science—What Makes Things Happen in the World around Me?
600-699	Applied Science—How Can I Control Nature?
700-799	Arts and Recreation—How Can I Enjoy My Spare Time?
800-899	Literature—What Are the Stories of Man's Great Deeds and Thoughts?
900-999	History—How Can I Record What Man Has Done?

2) 45 4x4" colored posterboard player cards, illustrated on page 168, with a number (1-45) on the back, but with no indication there as to the type of card. The front side should have a sentence, a definition, a phrase, or a subject concerning the above classes. (A suggested list of these follows, but they are not necessarily played in this order.)

(Materials list continues on page 168)

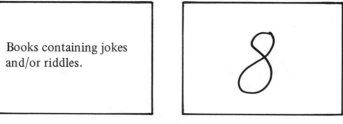

Player's card—front   Player's card—back

Books concerning the belief and worship of God or gods.

Books concerning the study of man, his relations, and institutions as a member of an organized community.

Books about all of the languages of the world, their dictionaries, and grammars.

Books that have many of the other nine Dewey Classifications in one book or a series of books.

Books containing information on witchcraft and strange happenings.

Books about travel to foreign countries.

Books about customs and/or holidays.

Books containing jokes and/or riddles.

Books containing folklore or fairy tales.

Books containing information on art and architecture.

Books about man's mind and thoughts.

Books containing information on the armed services.

Books about science—biology, chemistry, etc.

Books about nature—flowers, trees, etc.

Books with information on how to care for pets.

Books about capturing nature forever—photography.

3)   45 4x4" colored posterboard team leader cards, identical to the player cards on both sides, except that leader cards also have the classification number written on them beside the subject or class (this side faces the leader during play). These cards should be kept in two piles, one with the even card numbers and the other with the odd card numbers

Team leader cards are shown at the top of page 169.

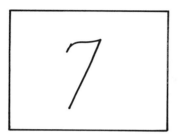

Team leader's or media
specialist's card—front
      Team leader's or media
specialist's card—back

4)   Large manila envelope (12x15") for the materials.

PROCEDURE:

1)   Divide the students into two evenly matched teams and choose a leader for each.

2)   Pass to the players all of the posterboard player cards, with numbers facing up. These remain up until one of those numbers is called or shown by the team leader (see step 5).

     (Some players may have more cards than others.)

3)   Place the 10 large Dewey division cards on a table or chalk tray.

4)   The team leaders are given a stack of team leader cards, one having odd numbers, the other having even numbers.

5)   One team leader picks up one of the small cards, showing only the sequence number to members of that team.

6)   The player having that sequence number takes that player card, turns it over, takes it to the 10 large division cards, and lays that card on or near the main class card that fits the player card.

7)   If it is correct, he or she leaves it there. If it is incorrect, the leader gives it back to the player and places the sequence number card back on the stack to be used again.

8)   Teams alternate turns.

9)   At the end of the game, the media specialist checks to see if all are correct and adds the points scored by each team.

■ ■ ■

$\diamondsuit$

DEWEY SHUFFLE

$\diamondsuit$

PURPOSE: To display a knowledge of the Dewey Decimal Classification System in order to independently locate books in the IMC/library.

To realize that each subject group contains much varied information.

GRADE LEVEL: Intermediate—6th grade

TIME: 50 minutes

NUMBER: Best played with a maximum of 16 students

METHOD OF CHECKING: Media specialist

MATERIALS:
1) Newspaper clippings (articles and pictures) representing as varied a field as possible; dry-mounted on colored paper; these are "Dewey Shuffle" cards.

2) 16 "Curious George Wants to Know about the Dewey Decimal Classification System" bookmarks.

3) Large manila envelope (16x20") for the materials.

PROCEDURE:
1) Divide the students into two evenly matched teams, place each team around a table, and choose leaders for each.

2) Place an even number of "Dewey Shuffle" cards on the tables around which team members are gathered.

3) The cards are to be sorted by the teams into stacks representing the different subject groups.

4) Check the stacks carefully to determine that all is correct (with the help of the bookmarks).

5) The team leader raises a hand when all is finished.

6) The media specialist will check stacks and determine the number of points that a team has scored.

7) Two players record what is in each stack.

8) In the next period, discuss all of the different categories found within each subject group.

■ ■ ■

PART IV

ROCKETING INTO REFERENCES:
Reference Books

What are reference books? In what section of the IMC/library are they found? Are they difficult to use? Why should we know something about them? Reference books provide information arranged in such a way that it can be located easily. They are not meant to be read through. They are usually not difficult to use. Once a student learns to check certain parts of a reference book—the table of contents, index, glossary, copyright date, and text—she or he will understand the purpose of the book and will find the needed information. However, in order to develop independent study habits, a student should be familiar with the basic types of reference books. Some of the basic tools to be found in an IMC/library are: 1) encyclopedias, 2) atlases, 3) dictionaries, 4) biographical dictionaries and directories, 5) indexes, 6) almanacs, and 7) handbooks-manuals.

Students should use reference books when some specific facts or information on a particular subject are needed. For example, what is the meaning of "demon"?— check an English-language dictionary for the answer. Who was Susan B. Anthony?— check a biographical dictionary for the answer. What is the state flower of Idaho?— check an encyclopedia or special states book for the answer. What is the longest river in the world?—check an almanac for the answer. The list could go on infinitely because of the variety of reference works to be found within an IMC/ library.

The games in this chapter are designed for students to become familiar with the many and varied types of reference works available in which to locate information. However, before using the games in this chapter, it would be wise to review how reference books are organized. The following AV materials would be a good way to spark discussion.

1) "How to Find Information in Reference Books" (*Your Library and Media Center: How to Get the Most from Them*; The Center for Humanities, Inc.; sound filmstrip; 10 minutes; color).

2) "What's in the Dictionary?" (*Using the Elementary School Library*; SVE; sound filmstrip; 16 minutes; color).

3) "How to Use the Encyclopedia" (*Using the Elementary School Library*; SVE; sound filmstrip; 14 minutes, color).

4) "How to Use Encyclopedias" (*Look It Up: How to Get Information*; Troll Associates; sound filmstrip; 10 minutes; color).

5) "Getting Acquainted with Sources of Information: Reference Books" (*How to Use the Library*; Educational Progress Corporation; audio cassette; Tape 10; 20 minutes).

6) "Getting Acquainted with Sources of Information: The Dictionary" (*How to Use the Library*; Educational Progress Corporation; audio cassette; Tape 8 [Part I] and Tape 9 [Part II]; 20 minutes each tape).

7) "Getting Acquainted with Sources of Information: The Encyclopedia" (*How to Use the Library*; Educational Progress Corporation; audio cassette; Tape 9 [Part I] and Tape 10 [Part II]; 20 minutes each tape).

WORD SEARCH

PURPOSE: To give students practice in locating simple words in dictionaries.

GRADE LEVEL: Primary—1st and 2nd grades

TIME: Form A—25 minutes
           Form B—25 minutes

NUMBER: Best played with a maximum of 16 students

METHOD OF CHECKING: Media specialist

MATERIALS:
   1)   1 dictionary for every student. A good one to start with is *My Picture
        Dictionary* (Ginn & Company) or the *Beginning to Read Picture
        Dictionary* (Follett Publishing Company). As students become pro-
        ficient with these, the *Golden Picture Dictionary* (Golden Press)
        becomes more of a challenge for them. All dictionaries should be the
        same, whatever is used.

PROCEDURE:

   Form A

   1)   Divide the students into two evenly matched teams and choose leaders
        for each.

   2)   Each student is given a dictionary.

   3)   Each team is to sit in a semi-circle on the floor, or use chairs,
        arranged alphabetically by first names. The person with the name
        closest to the beginning of the alphabet is first.

   4)   The media specialist chooses a number from 1 to 10, in order to
        determine team order of play. The team leaders are to guess a number
        between 1 and 10. The number that matches (or is closest to) the
        number that the media specialist has written down designates which
        team goes first.

   5)   The leader of the starting team stands in front of all of the players.
        She or he is to think of a word and tell it to the participants, who are
        all supposed to look for the word in their dictionaries.

(Procedures continue on page 174)

6) The leader is to pick a player from the opposing team to tell on what page the word is located.

7) If correct, that player scores a point and replaces the leader "up front" to think of a new word. If incorrect, the leader chooses someone from his or her own team to answer.

8) In each instance, except when a word is missed, the person "up front" will be directing the word to members of the opposing team.

9) Players will be scoring points both for themselves—one point for each correct answer—as well as for their teams.

10) The team with the most points at the end of the match will be the winners.

11) Game may be played one or more times, depending upon class interest and the need to learn how to search for words.

Form B

1) Go through steps 1 through 5 of Form A.

2) The leader of one team stands in front of all of the players, thinks of a word, uses it in a sentence, and tells the sentence to the participants.

3) All players are to determine the word and look for it in the dictionary.

4) The leader is to pick a player from the opposing team to tell on what page the word is located and to read the definition.

5) If correct, the player scores a point and replaces the leader "up front" to think of a new word to use in a sentence. If incorrect, the leader chooses someone from his own team to answer.

6) Steps 6 through 11 are the same as for Form A.

■ ■ ■

FIND THE LETTER

PURPOSE: To have students practice opening dictionaries to the proper alphabetical section.

GRADE LEVEL: Primary—2nd and 3rd grades

TIME: 25 minutes

NUMBER: Best played with a maximum of 16 students

METHOD OF CHECKING: Media specialist

MATERIALS:
1)   1 dictionary for every student; the same kind should be given to everyone.
2)   1 9x12" score card drawn on acetate paper:

SCORE CARD	
Team 1	Team 2

3)   Overhead projector and screen.
4)   1 Vis-a-Vis® pen.
5)   Damp paper towels to clean the score card at the end of the game.
6)   Large manila envelope (10x13") for the materials.

PROCEDURE:

1) Divide the students into two evenly matched teams and choose a leader for each.

2) Each student is given a dictionary.

3) Teams are to sit facing one another at tables or on the floor.

4) The media specialist chooses a number from 1 to 10, in order to determine team order of play. The team leaders are to guess a number between 1 and 10. The number that matches (or is closest to) the number that the media specialist has written down designates which team goes first.

5) The media specialist calls out a letter for one team—e.g., S.

6) The players on one team attempt to open their dictionaries to the proper section in one try (S, in this case).

7) For each player who finds the correct section in the first try, one point is scored for the team. The media specialist is to check the dictionaries and record scores on the score card.

8) The second team plays in the same fashion after a different letter has been called.

9) Play continues with the teams taking turns.

10) The team with the most points at the end of the match will win.

11) The game may be played one or more times, depending upon class interest and the need to learn to open to the correct section.

■ ■ ■

GUIDE WORD SORT

PURPOSE: To gain skill and speed in using the guide words in a dictionary.

GRADE LEVEL: Primary—3rd grade

TIME: 25 minutes

NUMBER: Best played with a maximum of 16 students

METHOD OF CHECKING: Media specialist

MATERIALS:
1) 16 9x12" oak-tag cards divided into three columns; this is the "Guide Word Sort Card":

Page in front	Guide words	Page behind

2) 16 3x1" "Guide Word Cards" to fit into the middle column, labeled as follows: cage—camp; take—tap; mine—miser; copy—corral; weed—wet; need—news; stir—story; arch—army; book—bow; dam—date; ebb—elf; fancy—file; gem—glory; help—high; jest—jump; left—lift.

(Materials list continues on page 178)

3) 256 2x2" colored posterboard word cards, divided into 16 sets of
    16 cards each, and labeled (one word to a card) as below in each of
    the categories in number 2 above:

need–news	arch–army	dam–date
neon	arm	dame
nearly	ache	damp
night	area	dab
no	around	daft
nap	agree	daily
nice	argue	dais
net	armor	dark
nickel	about	dank
necklace	at	dare
next	angle	dance
new	any	dart
neck	all	dash
neat	ark	daub
nest	arbor	day
never	apple	dawn
neutral	arctic	dead

stir–story	weed–wet	ebb–elf
stow	west	ear
stop	way	early
stay	well	each
still	weep	earth
stool	wick	ease
stood	were	echo
stout	worst	edit
stiff	went	edge
steel	want	egg
stone	where	eight
storm	with	elbow
strap	week	eject
stove	welt	elm
stitch	wish	ember
stock	weigh	emit
steal	was	end

fancy–file	help–high	left–lift
face	hard	land
fable	hack	lash
fail	half	lady
fair	hall	lace
fall	hand	last
far	hang	law
farm	here	lend
fang	hence	lens
fat	herd	legal
fast	hide	less
fill	hint	lick
fine	hinge	levy
first	hives	lime
fire	hole	like
flag	horn	live
flow	hex	list

gem–glory	jest–jump	book–bow
gain	jack	brad
gage	jade	boss
gape	jerk	boom
gasp	jam	both
gear	jar	bowl
gene	jig	boy
germ	join	bottle
get	jet	boxing
gill	jog	bit
ghost	joust	bound
giant	jolt	bingo
glow	junk	black
goal	jury	bin
grade	just	box
gore	jute	bite
grass	jut	boat

(List continues on page 180)

cage—camp	**mine—miser**
cafe	mint
came	mire
cactus	miner
cabin	mirror
cape	million
candy	milk
can	map
call	man
calf	master
calm	mink
cable	minute
cadet	must
camel	muddle
cake	more
camera	mister
chip	murder

take—tap	**copy—corral**
task	cost
tall	cork
table	correct
talk	can
tape	coop
tale	cool
take	cap
top	cape
tail	copy
tip	coral
taught	cord
tame	cover
thank	corn
tank	card
tangle	corner
tap	cougar

4)   Number each "Guide Word Card" (1-16), and then number each word card in a set to correspond with its guide card number.

5)   16 6x9" manila envelopes to keep the "Guide Word Card" and the word cards in; number them each on the outside to correspond to the numbers on the back of the card sets.

6)   Large manila envelope (16x20") for the materials.

PROCEDURE:

1) Each player is given a "Guide Word Sort Card" and an envelope with a "Guide Word Card" and 16 word cards inside.

2) The "Guide Word Card" is placed at the top of the middle column on the "Guide Word Sort Card," and indicates the guide words for that round.

3) The player must decide in which column to place the word. If it can be found between the guide words, it is placed in the middle column. If the word is not found between the guide words, it is placed in either the "page in front" or the "page behind" column.

4) When finished, the player raises a hand, and the media specialist checks the cards.

5) If correctly placed, the cards are returned to their envelope and a new envelope is chosen. Play continues in the same fashion until a player has completed two envelopes. When four have been completed, the player may help someone who is having trouble.

6) If incorrect, the player continues until all cards are correctly placed. When finished, the player files the cards back in their envelope and a new one is taken, as above.

7) On the first attempt, each player receives eight points if all cards are correctly placed. When a correction has to be made, the point value goes down to four points.

8) The individual with the most points at the end of play is declared winner.

■ ■ ■

FIND THAT PLACE

PURPOSE: To gain practice in identifying places on a map through the use of compass directions.

GRADE LEVEL: Primary—2nd and 3rd grades

TIME: Part I—25 minutes
             Part II—25 minutes

NUMBER: Best played with a maximum of 16 students

METHOD OF CHECKING: Media specialist

MATERIALS:
1) 16 pieces of 9x12" oak-tag, colored posterboard, or wrapping paper.
2) 16 pencils, crayons, or felt-tip markers.
3) 1 large piece (12x15") colored posterboard.
4) Large manila envelope (16x20") for the materials.

PROCEDURE:

Part I

1) Give each student a piece of paper (whatever kind chosen), and tell them to draw the outlines of the room.

2) The media specialist is to help in the location of north, so that the student can make that side of the map the top, then label south at the bottom, east on the right, and west on the left.

3) After this, fit in the doorways, windows, and the large pieces of furniture. If it is a plan of an IMC, fill in the tables, card catalog, book shelves, check-out desk or counter, and so on.

4) When the maps are finished, the media specialist selects the best one and dry-mounts it on a piece of colored posterboard, then laminates it. This serves as the gameboard for "Find That Place."

Part II

1) Divide the students into two evenly matched teams and choose a leader for each.

2) Give back to each player the map that person drew.

3) Each team is to sit in a semi-circle on the floor, or use chairs, alphabetizing by first names. The person with the name closest to the beginning of the alphabet is first.

4) The media specialist chooses a number from 1 to 10, in order to determine team order of play. The team leaders are to guess a number between 1 and 10. The number that matches (or is closest to) the number that the media specialist has written down designates which team goes first.

5) The leader of the starting team stands in front of all the players. He or she is to direct others to name the article of furniture, for example, southeast of the door, or 5 feet from the window, or west of the card catalog.

6) All players are to check the gameboard(s).

7) The leader is to pick a player from the opposing team to tell what that article of furniture is.

8) If correct, the player scores a point and replaces the leader "up front" to think of a new direction. If incorrect, the leader chooses someone from his or her own team to answer.

9) In each instance, except when a direction is missed, the person "up front" will be giving the direction to members of the opposing team.

10) Players will be scoring points for themselves—one point for each correct answer—as well as for their team.

11) The team with the most points at the end of the match will win.

■ ■ ■

SPIDER SCRAMBLE

PURPOSE: To gain practice in choosing among an encyclopedia, an atlas, and an almanac to answer a question.

GRADE LEVEL: Intermediate—5th and 6th grades

TIME: 30 minutes

NUMBER: Best played with a maximum of 16 students

METHOD OF CHECKING: Answer sheet

MATERIALS:
1)   4 "Spider Scramble" gameboards made from 16x22" colored posterboard:

2) Appropriate reference books, such as: *World Book Encyclopedia, World Almanac*(s) for different years, and *Hammond World Atlas.*

3) 16 markers (4 per gameboard).

4) 4 dice (1 die per gameboard).

5) 4 9x12" oak-tag answer sheets (1 per gameboard).

6) 96 3x4" colored posterboard cards with questions (24 per gameboard). Do not indicate the reference book to be used to answer questions. The following are the types of questions appropriate to each type of reference work:

Almanac

Who was the Grand National Champion in motorcycle racing in 1974?

Who was elected governor of Wyoming in the 1976 election?

How much salary does the president of the United States receive?

Which was the busiest airport in the world in 1977?

In what year was Ringo Starr born?

Where was Elton John born?

How many people were lost in the "Titanic" disaster?

Encyclopedia

How much milk does it take to make a pound of cheese?

Who discovered radium?

What is the difference between a band and an orchestra?

Who first used wallpaper?

Why are some roads called turnpikes?

How many eggs can a female tick lay?

How many bones are in the human foot?

How is cellophane made?

Who made the game of chess popular in the United States?

Atlas

Is any coffee grown in the United States?

Name one range of mountains in Alaska.

Name the five Great Lakes.

What is the largest country in South America?

What sea is north of Turkey?

What is the greatest amount of rainfall in South America?

(Materials list continues on page 186)

7) 12 3x4" cards that say "Spider Scramble" on them (3 per gameboard).

8) Large manila envelope (12x15") for the materials.

PROCEDURE:

1) The students are divided into four groups by counting off in fours, and each group is given a gameboard and related materials.

2) The students roll the die to determine the order of play, with highest score starting.

3) Question cards and "Spider Scramble" cards are shuffled together and placed face down on the "Spider Scramble" gameboard.

4) All players place markers at "start."

5) The starting student rolls the die and draws a card from the pile.

6) The student tells in which reference book to look for the answer. If correct, the player moves clockwise the number of spaces indicated on the die and places the card at the bottom of the pile.

7) If incorrect, the player does not move and the card is placed at the bottom of the pile. The other players may use the answer sheet to determine if a player answers correctly.

8) Players continue to take turns in this manner.

9) When a "Spider Scramble" card is drawn, the player calls out "Scramble," and all markers ahead of the marker of the student drawing the card must return to "start."

10) The first player to reach "finish" is the winner.

■ ■ ■

PURPOSE: To give students practice in locating information in encyclopedias.

GRADE LEVEL: Intermediate—5th and 6th grades

TIME: 25 minutes

NUMBER: Best played with a maximum of 16 students

METHOD OF CHECKING: Media specialist

MATERIALS:
1) 40 3x4" colored posterboard cards, each with different "encyclopedia" questions printed on them, as follows:

How did a pocket gopher get its name? (they have fur-lined pouches on the outside of their cheeks—*World Book Encyclopedia, Compton's, Britannica Jr.*)

Does a pecan grow on a tree? (yes—*World Book Encyclopedia, Compton's, Britannica Jr.*)

Where and what was the earliest known Christian sanctuary? (a private house in Dura, eastern Syria, A.D. 200—*World Book*)

Why is an aconite sometimes called monkshood? (because its flow resembles the hoods worn by monks—*World Book*)

Where are the ears of a cricket located? (on the inside of its front legs—*Compton's, World Book*)

Can fish hear? (yes—*World Book, Book of Knowledge, Compton's*)

How did Buffalo Bill (William Cody) get his nickname? (by killing over 4,000 buffalo in 18 months for workers building a western railroad—*World Book, Britannica Jr., Book of Knowledge, Compton's*)

What is smog? (a form of air pollution—*World Book, Book of Knowledge*)

How far can a rattlesnake strike? (it can strike little more than one-half the length of its body—*Britannica Jr., Compton's*)

(Materials list continues on page 188)

187

Can you tell a rattlesnake's age by the number of its rattles? (no—
World Book, Britannica Jr.)

Can the porcupine shoot its quills? (no—*World Book, Britannica Jr.,
Compton's*)

How often do our eyelids blink? (25 times per minute—*World Book,
Britannica Jr.*)

Is Irish moss a seaweed? (yes—*World Book*)

What is a paramecium? (a tiny one-celled animal that can hardly be seen
without a microscope—*World Book*)

How does Roquefort cheese get its blue-veined appearance? (penicillan
mold—*World Book*)

What animal does a panda resemble? (giant panda: bears; Red panda:
raccoon—*World Book, Britannica Jr.*)

What is isinglass? (purest form of animal gelatin—*World Book*)

What makes the holes in Swiss cheese? (bacteria that give off gas—
Compton's)

What is the Rosetta Stone? (a stone which gave the key to the long-
forgotten language of ancient Egypt—*World Book*)

Of what use is a camel's hump? (to carry a built-in food supply, a
large lump of fat that provides energy for the animal—*World
Book, Britannica Jr., Book of Knowledge, Compton's*)

What bird makes a raft for a nest? (grebes build floating nests on rafts
of decaying vegetation in lakes and ponds—*World Book,
Compton's*)

From what material do the Adélie penguins build nests? (pebbles and
the bones of their ancestors—*Book of Knowledge*)

Is it correct to call all insects bugs? (no—*World Book, Britannica Jr.*)

What is a newspaper "morgue"? (its research library—*World Book,
Compton's*)

What is an ant lion? (it is the larve [young] of an adult insect that
looks like a dragonfly—*World Book*)

How do ants communicate with one another? (by tapping with their
antennae; scent trails; sounds—rubbing one part of their armor-
like body against another [striculation]—*Compton's, Book of
Knowledge*)

The Osage Indians are located in what area of the United States?
(the Midwest and in Oklahoma—*World Book*)

What is an Osage orange? (a thorny tree that can be used as a wire hedge; its fruit is not good for humans, only animals—*World Book, Britannica Jr.*)

Does a wasp see an entire object at one time? (no, everything is broken into small bits—*World Book*)

Which wasp is the only one to be a tool-using insect? (digger wasp—*Britannica Jr., Compton's*)

How fast can a duck fly? (up to 70 miles per hour—*Compton's*)

How far will a radio wave go in one second? (186,282 miles per second—*World Book, Compton's, Britannica Jr.*)

How does a fish breathe? (it gulps water through the mouth and pumps it over its gills to get the oxygen—*World Book, Britannica Jr., Compton's, Book of Knowledge*)

What gives fireworks their color? (special chemicals: sodium compounds—yellow; strontium compounds—red; copper and barium compounds—blue and green—*World Book, Compton's, Britannica Jr., Book of Knowledge*)

What is unusual about the lionfish? (its fins look like bird feathers and are as sharp as needles; it gives off a poison; it uses its fins to attack other fish and may even attack skin divers—*World Book*)

What is the nickname for Affenpinscher? (monkey dog—*World Book*)

What is the color of a live lobster? (dark green or dark blue—*World Book, Compton's, Britannica Jr., Book of Knowledge*)

What are "gunny sacks" made of? (coarse jute cloth used mainly to make burlap bags and sacks—*World Book*)

Which can run faster—a man or a hippopotamus? (on land, hippos can run as fast as a human being, about 20 miles [32 kilometers] per hour—*World Book, Book of Knowledge, Compton's*)

2) Various sets of encyclopedias, preferably the ones mentioned above; or else ones from which questions and answers have been drawn.

3) Large manila envelope (9x12") for the materials.

PROCEDURE:
1) Divide the students into two evenly matched teams.

2) Place the question cards face down on a table, 20 for each team.

3) Each player chooses a card with a question that can be answered by looking in an encyclopedia.

(Procedures continue on page 190)

4)   When the information is located, the player either writes the answer on a sheet of paper or shows the media specialist the correct answer, and then chooses a second card.

5)   When two questions' answers have been successfully located, a player may help someone else on the team.

6)   The first team to answer all of their questions correctly wins the game.

7)   For each correct answer, the player also scores one point.

■ ■ ■

SCRAMBLED REFERENCE

PURPOSE: To familiarize students with such various reference works as *Bartlett's Familiar Quotations,* the *Trivia Encyclopedia,* and *Early American Costume,* and their descriptions.

GRADE LEVEL: Intermediate—5th and 6th grades

TIME: 45 minutes

NUMBER: Best played with a maximum of 16 students

METHOD OF CHECKING: Media specialist

MATERIALS:

1)   48 2x6" colored posterboard cards, divided into 16 sets with three cards per set. On each card should be a reference title and its description formed like jigsaw pieces. [For a listing of single-volume reference books and their descriptions, see Appendix II, page 239.]

   Number all sets (1-16), making sure that each piece of a card has the same number.

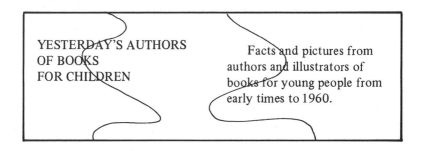

2)   16 6x9" manila envelopes in which to keep the puzzle pieces, numbered on the outside to correspond to the number on the back of the puzzle pieces inside. In each envelope, there should be 12 jigsaw pieces all numbered alike (1-16, depending on the set).

3)   Small cardboard box for the materials.

PROCEDURE:

1) Divide the students into two evenly matched teams.

2) A team leader is chosen and becomes the first player on that team. Other team members line up behind the leader.

3) The first player on each team is given an envelope with a set of three reference titles and their matching descriptions.

4) The jigsaw pieces are to be placed on a table or floor to match.

5) Each player must match the jigsaw pieces of all cards, then shuffle them and replace in the envelope, and pass to the person behind.

6) While the second players are matching their cards, the first players receive another set of cards.

7) This procedure continues with the first players receiving as many envelopes as there are players on the team. If there are eight team members, each player matches 24 cards (3 sets per envelope).

8) The team that finishes first is the winner and each member receives 4 points. Each member of the losing team receives 2 points.

9) The media specialist, throughout the entire game, should circulate among the players to see that everything is proceeding correctly.

■ ■ ■

WHAT'S MY BOOK???

PURPOSE: To gain skill in differentiating among the different types of single-volume reference books.

GRADE LEVEL: Intermediate—5th and 6th grades

TIME: 50 minutes

NUMBER: Best played with a maximum of 16 students

METHOD OF CHECKING: Media specialist

MATERIALS:
1) 16 9x12" oak-tag cards with the titles of different single-volume reference books on them. [For a listing of single-volume reference books, see Appendix II, page 239.]

2) Yarn, to be attached to each card through holes punched in the upper corners, enough to allow the card to be hung around a student's neck (12-14" long).

3) One die.

4) Large manila envelope (12x15") for the materials.

PROCEDURE:
1) Divide students into two teams and choose a leader for each.

2) The leaders roll the die to determine the starting team (Team A). The teams form two lines and sit facing the media specialist.

3) The media specialist shows a card to Team A and hangs it on the back of the first member of Team A, who then stands facing the two teams.

4) Each member of Team B asks a question of the person from Team A. The questions must be able to be answered with "yes" or "no." (For example: Can the president's salary be found in this book?)

5) Team B attempts to guess the title of the book from the information gained from the answers to their questions.

6) For every question answered correctly by the Team A member, that team scores a point.

(Procedures continue on page 194)

7) When Team B guesses the title of the book, 10 points are scored and Team A gets a turn. If Team B does not guess the title of the book, Team A scores 10 points. The team is given three minutes to guess each answer.

8) Play continues in this manner, with teams alternating turns.

9) The team with the most points at the end of the game wins.

■ ■ ■

FORTY QUESTIONS

PURPOSE: To help students understand the types of information that can be found within different types of reference books.

GRADE LEVEL: Intermediate—6th grade

TIME: Part I—50 minutes
               Part II—25 minutes
               Part III—50 minutes

NUMBER: Best played with a maximum of 16 students

METHOD OF CHECKING: Media specialist

MATERIALS:
1)   10 single-volume reference books such as:

        Bartlett's Familiar Quotations
        Famous First Facts
        Brewer's Dictionary of Phrase and Fable
        Dictionary of Mythical Places
        The Trivia Encyclopedia
        National Geographic Index, 1947-1976
        Stories of the States
        In Other Words: A Junior Thesaurus
        Who's Who in Greek and Roman Mythology
        Junior Book of Authors

2)   Dittoed sheets listing the ten single-volume reference titles used; one for each student.

3)   Dittoed sheets listing only a blank for the title, but giving a concise description of each of the books used:

        _____ : a collection of quotations
                                           and their sources.

4)   Master list of questions and answers, dry-mounted to a piece of colored posterboard; the following types of questions work well:

(Materials list continues on page 196)

From what source did the following quotation come? "Some are born great, some achieve greatness, and some have greatness thrust upon 'em" (*Bartlett's Familiar Quotations*)

What was the name of the first baseball team? *(Famous First Facts)*

What is an 'oatin pipe'? (*Brewer's Dictionary of Phrase and Fable*)

What do the Japanese believe about Ama? (*Dictionary of Mythical Places*)

Who is Fritz? (*The Trivia Encyclopedia*)

In what issue of a magazine would you find an article on Cartier, Jacques? (*National Geographic Index*)

What is the nickname for Alabama? (*Stories of the States*)

What is another word for humorous? (*In Other Words: A Junior Thesaurus*)

Who were the Furies? (*Who's Who in Greek and Roman Mythology*)

What is the pen name for Margaret Wise Brown? (*Junior Book of Authors*)

From what source came this advise, "In baiting a mousetrap with cheese, always leave room for the mouse"? (*Bartlett's Familiar Quotations*)

When was basketball invented? (*Famous First Facts*)

What does the 'Curse of Scotland' mean? (*Brewer's Dictionary of Phrase and Fable*)

What is Asgard? (*Dictionary of Mythical Places*)

Who invented Coca-Cola? (*The Trivia Encyclopedia*)

In what issue of a magazine would you find an article on cobras? (*National Geographic Index*)

What does Vermont mean? (*Stories of the States*)

What is another word for bravery? (*In Other Words: A Junior Thesaurus*)

Who was Jupiter? (*Who's Who in Greek and Roman Mythology*)

What book by Marguerite Henry won the ALA Award in 1949? (*Junior Book of Authors*)

From what source did the following quotation come, "Children of yesterday, heirs of tomorrow"? (*Bartlett's Familiar Quotations*)

When was the first revolving cylinder gun made? (*Famous First Facts*)

Why is the Garden of the Hesperides famous in Greek Mythology? (*Dictionary of Mythical Places*)

What was the real name of 'Billy the Kid'? (*The Trivia Encyclopedia*)

In what issue of a magazine would you find an article on falconry? (*National Geographic Index*)

What does Colorado mean? (*Stories of the States*)

What is another word for sound? (*In Other Words: A Junior Thesaurus*)

Who was Nemesis? (*Who's Who in Greek and Roman Mythology*)

A. A. Milne wrote what famous story about a little bear? (*Junior Book of Authors*)

From what source did the following quotation come, "The hand that rocks the cradle is the hand that rules the world"? (*Bartlett's Familiar Quotations*)

Who was the first president to travel underwater in a captured enemy submarine? (*Famous First Facts*)

What is Mirkwood? (*Dictionary of Mythical Places*)

Who was the Red Baron? (*The Trivia Encyclopedia*)

In what issue of a magazine would you find an article on jellyfish? (*National Geographic Index*)

What is the state flower of Hawaii? (*Stories of the States*)

What is another word for special? (*In Other Words: A Junior Thesaurus*)

Who is Ganymede? (*Who's Who in Greek and Roman Mythology*)

In what city was Elizabeth Coatsworth born? (*Junior Book of Authors*)

What is a billabong? (*Brewer's Dictionary of Phrase and Fable*)

What is a griffin? (*Brewer's Dictionary of Phrase and Fable*)

5) A coin of any denomination.

6) Master sheet, for the use of the media specialist, listing the titles and concise descriptions of the reference books used; dry-mounted to a piece of colored posterboard.

   For example:

   Dictionary of Mythical Places: an alphabetically arranged dictionary of mythical, legendary, and famous places that briefly describes the origin, location, and major characteristics of each place.

   (For a listing of single-volume reference books and descriptions, see Appendix II, page 239.)

7) Large manila envelope (10x13") for the materials.

PROCEDURE:

Part I

1) Each student is given a copy of the list of 10 titles and must make a good description of each reference work by looking through it. They should take notes.

2) Students may work in pairs and exchange the descriptions in preparation for an oral report.

3) After each presentation, the class and the media specialist ask questions to clarify the description of the reference.

4) Students are to study their sheets in preparation for Part II.

Part II

1) Each student gets a dittoed copy of the concise descriptions of the reference works (see number 3 of materials list).

2) Start with an oral drill on the reference works, and have the students fill in the blanks as each title is guessed.

3) For each correct answer, one point is given.

4) Remind students to bring both the list of titles and the sheet of descriptions for Part III.

Part III

1) Divide the students into two evenly matched teams and choose a leader for each.

2) The team leader whose last name is closest to the beginning of the alphabet is first to call "heads" or "tails" and flips a coin. Whichever team's leader calls the flip correctly is first.

3) The media specialist asks various questions (as above), for which team members must name the reference containing the answer.

4) Each team's leader will choose which team members will answer which questions.

5) If the answer is correct, the student receives two points; if not, the opposing team has a chance to correctly answer the question and then take an additional turn.

6) The team with the most points wins.

■ ■ ■

REFERENCE FLIP

PURPOSE: To gain practice in deciding which reference book to use.

GRADE LEVEL: Intermediate—5th and 6th grades

TIME: 50 minutes

NUMBER: Best played with a maximum of 16 students

METHOD OF CHECKING: Part A—self-checking; Part B—media specialist

MATERIALS:
  1) One box for each reference flip. Flat nylon-stocking boxes or ditto master boxes work well for this game.

  2) 16 pictures from magazines that will clearly show if a piece is misplaced when they are cut into jigsaw puzzles.

  3) 16 questions concerning single-volume references for each box.

  4) Appropriately sized large cardboard box for storage of the reference flip boxes.

  5) Ditto questions (from Step 3) on tagboard sheets cut to fit the boxes. (If 16 different sets of questions are desired, type the questions on oak-tag and laminate them.) Number the questions.

  6) Ditto the titles of the single-volume references on tagboard in the order that matches the numbered order of the answers to the questions on the question sheets (if 16 different answer sheets are needed, they may be written or typed individually).

  Illustration of question sheet and answer sheet appears on page 200.

  7) Glue the answer sheet to the back of a picture (from Step 2) so that the picture is visible on one side and the answers are visible on the other side.

(Materials list continues on page 200)

1. In what book would you find the quotation, "I can resist everything except temptation"?	9.
2.	10.
3.	11.
4.	12.
5.	13.
6.	14.
7.	15.
8.	16.

Question Sheet

1. *Bartlett's*	9.
2.	10.
3.	11.
4.	12.
5.	13.
6.	14.
7.	15.
8.	16.

Answer Sheet

8) As with a jigsaw puzzle, cut the sheet so that *each answer is a complete separate piece.*

9) A question sheet is glued to the inside of each flat box *cover.*

10) The inside *bottom* of this "Reference Flip Box" is ruled to correspond with the answer sheet and numbered. [See illustration at the top of page 201.]

11) The cut pieces of the answer sheet are stored inside the box.

PROCEDURE:

Part A

1) Each student is given a "Reference Flip Box."

2) The student empties the separate answer pieces and turns the cover over to see the inside where the questions are located.

1.	9.
2.	10.
3.	11.
4.	12.
5.	13.
6.	14.
7.	15.
8.	16.

[Inside bottom of box]

3) The player reads the first question silently and checks through the answer pieces for the single-volume reference book that would be consulted.

4) The answer piece is placed in the space numbered 1 in the bottom of the box.

5) The player arranges all of the answer pieces in this manner while answering the questions.

6) When all of the spaces in the bottom of the box are filled, the player places the top of the box—top side down—in the bottom of the box and, holding firmly, flips the box over.

7) The player carefully removes the bottom of the box and if all answers are correct, the picture should be complete on the top of the box.

8) If the picture is not in order, some answers are incorrect and the player must check the work to find the correct answer. The easiest way to accomplish this is to do the answers over.

Part B

1) When the picture is complete, the player may go to the single-volume references and answer the questions using the correct volume.

2) For each correct answer, the player scores five points. (The media specialist is to check the answers for accuracy.)

3) The player with the most points wins.

■ ■ ■

DIGGING IN

PURPOSE: To demonstrate the ability to "dig" information from specific reference works.

GRADE LEVEL: Intermediate—6th grade

TIME: Part I—50 minutes
           Part II—25 minutes
           Part III—50 minutes

NUMBER: Best played with a maximum of 16 students

METHOD OF CHECKING: Media specialist

MATERIALS:
    1)   10 single-volume reference books such as:

           Guinness Book of World Records
           Book of Marvels
           Children's Literature Review
           Early American Costume
           Word Origins and Their Romantic Stories
           Our Country's National Parks
           Third Book of Junior Authors
           Index to Children's Poetry
           Newbery and Caldecott Medal Books, 1966-1975
           Roget's Thesaurus

    2)   Dittoed sheets listing the ten single-volume reference titles used; one for each student.

    3)   40 3x4" colored posterboard cards with single-volume reference questions printed on them, such as the following:

           How much did the heaviest newborn child weigh? (24 lbs. 4 oz.)

           Who is Judy Blume? (an American author who writes mainly about suburban adolescents)

           What is the highest waterfall in the world? (Yosemite Falls)

           What did a little boy's costume look like in 1810-1820? (suit with frilly blouse)

What does fantasy mean? (making visible)

In which national park would Frozen Niagara be found? (Mammoth Cave National Park)

Which of Lloyd Alexander's books won the Newbery Medal for 1969? (*The High King*)

Where was Robert Hofsinde born? (Denmark)

Who wrote "Perhaps You'd Like to Buy a Flower?" (Emily Dickinson)

What is another word for zest? (relish, guesto)

What is the price of the most expensive car in the world? ($500,000)

For what book did Madeleine L'Engle win the Newbery Medal in 1963? (*A Wrinkle in Time*)

Which two mountains are described in one of the reference books as "the most beautiful" in the world? (Popocatepetal and Ixtaccehauate)

What did a young lady's dress look like in 1720-1740? (printed linen with a bodice fitted over a corset in front and a back fullness resembling a bustle)

What does ink mean? (burned in)

In which national park would the snowy egret be found? (Everglades National Park)

What was the first book that Bill Peet wrote? (*Hubert's Hair-Raising Adventure*)

In what poetry book would the entire poem "Under the Sun" be located? (*Yesterday and Today*)

In what year did *Always Room for One More* win the Caldecott Award? (1966)

What is the longest word in the English language? (floccinaucinihili-pilification, meaning the action of estimating as worthless)

What award did E. B. White win in 1970? (Laura I. Wilder Award)

Describe the uniform of a Dutch military man of the 1620-1630s (a doublet and breeches under a sleeveless military jerkin made of leather)

What does buccaneers mean? (a grill for cooking)

Which national park has the famous "Cliff Palace" as part of its attractions? (Mesa Verde National Park)

(Materials list continues on page 204)

Why did Mary Calhoun write her *Katie John* books? (they resulted from happy memories of the big old house in which she grew up)

What poem did Aaron Hill write? ("Grasp It Like a Man")

Arrow to the Sun is about what American Indian tribe? (Pueblo)

What is another word for feeling? (sensation)

Who has the most tattoos? (Vivian 'Sailor Joe' Simmons)

What is the name of the city that rose from the dead? (Pompeii)

What type of stories does Beverly Cleary write? (humorous)

Describe an American hunting outfit of the early 18th century (linen shirts or smocks, belt, shoulder strap, cartridge pouch, deerskin Indian leggings over the knee breeches)

What does daisy mean? (the eye of the day)

In which national park would Ribbon Falls be located? (Grand Canyon National Park)

Why did Carol Kendall write the *Grammage Cup*? (she found the Minnipins kicking around in her head and they wound up in her fantasy)

Helen Wing wrote a poem about what certain insect? (cricket)

Robert O'Brien, who wrote *Mrs. Frisby and the Rats of Nimh*, is the pen name for what author? (Robert Leslie Conly)

What is another word for universe? (cosmos)

What is another word for habit? (custom)

4) A coin of any denomination.

5) Master sheet, for the use of the media specialist, listing both the titles and concise descriptions of the reference books used; dry-mounted to a piece of colored posterboard. (For example, see "Forty Questions," page 197.)

[For a listing of single-volume reference books and descriptions, see Appendix II, page 239.]

6) One ditto sheet for each student, with concise descriptions of the references and with blank spaces on the left margin for the title (as in "Forty Questions").

Illustration appears at the top of page 205.

7) Large manila envelope (10x13") for the materials.

Example:

_____ : this book is filled with
pictures of the world's cities, mountains, temples, and maps
to show where they are located. The information is related in
story-book style.

PROCEDURE:

Part I

1) Each student is given a copy of the list of 10 titles and must make a
good description of each reference work by looking through it. They
should take notes.

2) Students may work in pairs and exchange the descriptions in preparation for an oral report.

3) Students to sit in a circle on the floor and exchange answers.

4) After each presentation, the class and media specialist ask questions
to clarify the description of the reference.

5) Students are to study their sheets in preparation for Part II.

Part II

1) Give each student a dittoed copy of concise descriptions of the reference books, with blank spaces on the left margin for the titles.

2) Start with an oral drill on the references, and have the students fill in
the blanks as each title is guessed.

3) For each correct answer one point is given.

4) Remind students to bring both the list of titles and the sheet of descriptions for Part III.

Part III

1) Students are to take the first five minutes to look over their papers.

2) Divide the students into two evenly matched teams.

3) Place the question cards face down on a table.

4) Each player chooses a card with a question that can be answered by
looking in a single-volume reference book.

(Procedures continue on page 206)

5) When the information is located, the player either writes the answer on a sheet of paper, or shows the media specialist the correct answer; the player then chooses a second card.

6) When three answers have been successfully located, a player may help someone else on the team.

7) The first team to answer all of their questions wins the game.

8) For each correct answer, the player scores two points.

[Note: One variation is to have several "digging in" sessions after each four or five tools are presented and discussed.]

■ ■ ■

PART V

THE MESSAGE IN THE MACHINE:
AV Equipment

Given the technological explosion within recent years, it is evident that man is certain to become more dependent on machines in the future. Videotaping and home computers are realities, available to the general public. Who knows what the future will bring? We can be sure that there will definitely be more machines in our lives. Machines (or hardware) have only been accepted grudgingly as part of IMCs, yet students are intrigued with hardware and are particularly adept at developing skills in this area. Being media-oriented, students today are thrilled to use media equipment. Two aids that can be of help in introducing this unit are:

1. "Care of Non-Book Materials: Loops and Tapes" (*Use the Library Effectively*; Creative Visuals; transparencies, color).

2. "Care of Non-Book Materials: Filmstrips and Records" (*Use the Library Effectively*; Creative Visuals; transparencies; color).

PUZZLING SKELETON

PURPOSE: To gain skill in recognizing AV equipment and software.

GRADE LEVEL: Primary—1st and 2nd grades

TIME: 25 minutes

NUMBER: Best played with a maximum of 16 students

METHOD OF CHECKING: Media specialist

MATERIALS:
1)   Flannel board (26x36") divided in half by a piece of yarn glued down the center.

2)   2 felt skeletons, each cut into 8 pieces. Skeletons should be approximately 18" tall.

3)   16 4x6" colored posterboard cards with pictures of AV equipment and software pasted onto them; the following should be pictured:

cassette tape recorder	filmstrip
phonodisc	language master
record player	TV
audio tape	overhead projector
head set	transparency
film loop	audio flashcard
film loop projector	16mm movie projector
16mm film	filmstrip projector

4)   Large manila envelope (12x15") for the materials.

PROCEDURE:
1)   Divide students into two teams and choose a leader for each.

2)   The teams form two lines and sit in front of the flannel board.

3)   The media specialist chooses a number from 1 to 10, in order to determine team order of play.

4) The team leaders are to guess a number between 1 and 10. The number that matches (or is closest to) the number that the media specialist has written down designates which team goes first. Thereafter, teams alternate turns.

5) The media specialist shows a card to the first player of the starting team.

6) The player must correctly identify the item pictured on the card.

7) If correct, the player is given one piece of the team's skeleton, which is placed on that team's side of the flannel board.

8) If the first answer is incorrect, the other team may gain a piece of their skeleton by answering correctly.

9) If neither team is correct, no one receives a skeleton part.

10) The team that completes its skeleton wins, and each team member receives two points.

■ ■ ■

SQUIRMY WORM

PURPOSE: To gain skill in handling basic AV software and in using basic AV vocabulary.

GRADE LEVEL: Primary—1st grade through 3rd grade

TIME: 25 minutes

NUMBER: Best played with a maximum of 16 students

METHOD OF CHECKING: Media specialist

MATERIALS:
    1)   One flannel board (26x36").
    2)   2 felt "Squirmy Worm" heads (3" in diameter).

    3)   20 felt circles (3" in diameter).

4) 20 3x4" colored posterboard cards with instructions or questions on them. Some samples are:

> Show the way to roll up a filmstrip.
>
> Show how to start a tape recorder.
>
> Show how to handle a phonodisc and place it on the record player.
>
> Start the record player.
>
> What is software?

5) Various pieces of hardware and software needed to follow the instructions that are on the cards.

6) Large manila envelope (10x13") for the materials.

PROCEDURE:

1) Divide the group into two teams.

2) The teams form 2 lines and sit facing the flannel board, which has the two "Squirmy Worm" heads on it.

3) The media specialist chooses the team to start and reads a card.

4) The first member of that team follows the instructions or answers the question correctly.

5) If correct, the player receives a circle to add to the "Squirmy Worm" that represents that team, attempting to create a body for the worm.

6) If the first answer is incorrect, the other team gets a chance to add a circle to their "Squirmy Worm" by responding correctly.

7) If neither team responds correctly, the media specialist demonstrates or answers correctly; no circles are given.

8) Play continues in the above manner, with teams alternating turns. If all the cards are used before the game ends, the cards are shuffled and used again.

9) The team with the longest "Squirmy Worm" wins.

■ ■ ■

SCRAMBLES

PURPOSE: To gain familiarity with AV vocabulary and definitions.

GRADE LEVEL: Intermediate—5th and 6th grades

TIME: 45 minutes

NUMBER: Best played with a maximum of 16 students

METHOD OF CHECKING: Self-checking

MATERIALS:
1)   2 overhead projectors.

2)   A table.

3)   A screen or a piece of white paper 4'x5' taped on a blackboard or wall.

4)   56 6x9" manila envelopes.

5)   56 2x12" strips of acetate paper with audiovisual vocabulary words and definitions written on them with a Sharpie® pen; divide them into 2 sets. The following can be used on the strips (use each twice):

    audio cassette—a cassette cartridge with recording tape on it.

    audio flashcard—a card with recording tape on the back to be used with the language master.

    cassette recorder—a portable tape recorder, powered by AC or battery.

    Dukane projector—a projector that projects a sound filmstrip with a provision for a cassette or record.

    film loop—8mm film about 1/3 inch or 8mm wide.

    film loop projector—a projector using a prepared 8mm film cartridge.

    filmstrip—35mm film approximately 1½ inches wide.

    filmstrip projector—a device for projecting the images on 35mm film in vertical sequence.

    headset—speakers in a form that fit over a student's ears and plug into a listening station.

language master—a machine in which audio flash cards are used. The student may record or listen to pre-recorded cards.

listening center—a table or an area where students use a tape recorder or record player with a headset to hear a pre-recorded story.

model—a copy of an object.

opaque materials—materials that light can pass through, but that cannot be seen through themselves—book pages, maps, and so on.

opaque projector—a device that projects images from print materials.

overhead projector—a device to display images prepared on transparencies.

phonodisc—a record.

realia—real things, samples, or specimens.

record player—a machine that reproduces the sound on records.

reel of audio tape—a recording tape to be used with a reel-to-reel tape recorder.

reel-to-reel tape recorder—a tape recorder that takes a reel of audio tape that must be threaded.

16mm film—movie film approximately 2/3-inch or 16mm wide.

16mm projector—a device to project the images on 16mm film.

slide—35mm photographic film that is placed in mounts.

slide projector—a device that projects the images on slides.

study print—a picture.

television monitor—TV set to play recorded video tapes.

transparency—an image on clear plastic.

video tape—a recording tape that records both sound and picture.

6) An appropriately sized box to store the materials.

PROCEDURE:

1) Cut the individual words in each definition apart, and place each definition's parts in a separate envelope.

2) Number both sets (1-28) so that corresponding numbered envelopes contain the same definitions.

3) Divide the students into two evenly matched teams.

4) The teams form two lines and sit on the floor facing the screen and the table with the two overhead projectors.

(Procedures continue on page 214)

5) The media specialist gives the first player on each team envelope number 1.

6) Each student walks to the table, empties the envelope, and arranges the words into a sentence on the overhead projector.

7) When the sentence forms the definition of a vocabulary word, the student returns the pieces to the envelope, gives it to the media specialist, and takes the second envelope to the next player, who then takes a turn. The player who has completed a turn sits at the end of the line.

8) The first team to finish all of the definitions wins the game.

■ ■ ■

██

CLIPPING CONTEST

██

PURPOSE: To gain practice in recognizing AV definitions.

GRADE LEVEL: Intermediate—5th and 6th grades

TIME: 25 minutes

NUMBER: Best played with a maximum of 16 students

METHOD OF CHECKING: Media specialist

MATERIALS:
1) 56 definition cards made from 3x4" colored posterboard, with the definitions from "Scrambles," page 212, written on them (2 sets of 28 cards).
2) 56 clip-type clothespins with the vocabulary words that are defined written on them with magic marker (2 sets of 28).
3) 14 manila envelopes (9x12"); 4 definitions and their 4 matching clothespins are placed in each envelope.
4) 2 small boxes (7 envelopes in each box).
5) A table.

PROCEDURE:
1) The group is divided into two teams.
2) The teams form two lines and sit facing the table.
3) The boxes are placed on the table.
4) When the media specialist says, "go," a person on each team walks to the table, removes one envelope from the box, and empties the definition cards and clothespins on the table.
5) Each student matches the clothespin word to the definition by clipping the clothespin to the definition card.
6) When finished, the student raises a hand and the media specialist checks the cards.

(Procedures continue on page 216)

7) If incorrect, the student rearranges the clothespins until they are on the correct definitions.

8) If correct, the student takes the clothespin off of the cards, places the materials in the envelope, and puts the envelope in the box.

9) The student then tags the next teammate to take a turn. The student who has completed a turn sits at the end of the line.

10) The team that finishes first wins.

■ ■ ■

PURPOSE: To gain practice in learning the definitions of AV software and hardware.

GRADE LEVEL: Intermediate—5th and 6th grades

TIME: 25 minutes

NUMBER: Best played with a maximum of 16 students.

METHOD OF CHECKING: Media specialist

MATERIALS:

1) 1 "Around the World" board. This can be drawn on a blackboard by using a piece of string as a compass or it can be made of posterboard, then laminated. In either case, the board is a circle at least 1 foot in diameter, with an outer ring that is divided into sections. (Determining the number of sections requires careful figuring, as words are to be filled in letter by letter, disregarding hyphens. But each word must *begin* with the last letter of the preceding word—e.g., loo-p-honodisc— so first write them all in a row, overlapping end/initial letters as they will be used; *then* count the number of spaces needed—one to each letter.) Place small numbers in those slots wherein a word should end/ begin, as in this filled-in example:

(Materials list continues on page 218)

The desired result here is a circle surrounded by a ring that is divided into precisely the number of sections needed for the letters of the AV terms (as they are run together for this game):

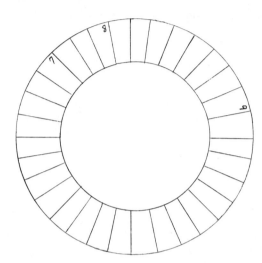

Using the words listed below would require 106 sections (again, disregarding hyphens).

2) 1 Vis-a-Vis® pen and paper towels, or chalk and eraser, as appropriate for the board.

3) 10 world chips (2" posterboard circles with the shapes of continents drawn on them).

4) 10 3x4" colored posterboard cards with the definitions of the words to be used printed on them. Cards must be numbered on the reverse side in the order in which they are to appear on the gameboard. (For the definitions, refer to "Scrambles," page 212.) Additional cards with different word sequences on them can be made. The end of the last word and the beginning of the first need not match if this can't be done. Example:

filmstrip projector—1	reel-to-reel—6
realia—2	loop—7
audio cassettes—3	phonodisc—8
study prints—4	cassette recorder—9
slide projector—5	record player—10

5) Large manila envelope to hold the materials.

PROCEDURE:

1) Divide the group into two teams by counting off in twos.

2) Attach the gameboard to a wall or blackboard.

3) The media specialist keeps the cards and world chips.

4) The teams form two lines and sit facing the gameboard.

5) The media specialist explains that all of the words on the gameboard begin with the last letter of the previous word, so play will continue until the circle is complete and the teams have gone "Around the World."

6) The media specialist draws the first card and reads the definition.

7) The first player who raises a hand comes to the gameboard and writes the word that matches that definition beginning in the space numbered one.

8) If correct, the player is given a world chip.

9) If incorrect, the other team has a chance to gain a chip by giving the correct answer. If neither team answers correctly, the media specialist writes in the correct word and no chips are given.

10) The team with the most world chips wins.

■ ■ ■

CINCH

PURPOSE: To match pictures of AV software and hardware.

GRADE LEVEL: Intermediate—5th and 6th grades

TIME: 25 minutes

NUMBER: Best played with a maximum of 16 students

METHOD OF CHECKING: Self-checking

MATERIALS:
1) 224 3x4" colored posterboard "Cinch" cards (for 4 packs) with pictures of hardware and software on them. One pack contains 56 cards, 2 for each of the 28 suggested pieces of software and hardware. (See "Scrambles," page 212, for the list of software and hardware.)

2) Large manila envelope (12x15") for the materials.

PROCEDURE:
1) Divide the class into groups of four students.

2) Each group is given a set of "Cinch" cards.

3) The cards are shuffled and dealt to the students.

4) Each student leaves his or her cards face down.

5) Any left over cards are placed face up in a pile in the center.

6) When play begins, all players turn any card up at the same time and form a second pile of face-up cards in front of themselves; players must turn up their cards away from themselves so that all can see the cards simultaneously.

7) When a player sees a card identical to one already turned up on top of any face-up pile, he or she says "Cinch" and places a hand flat on that pile.

8) The student receives both piles concerned and places them beneath the face-down pile already his or hers.

9) If anyone slaps by mistake, that person loses all face-up cards, which are then placed under the center pile.

10) The student with the most cards correctly matched at the end of the game is the winner.

■ ■ ■

MEMORY

PURPOSE: To become familiar with AV software and hardware and which software to use with the appropriate hardware.

GRADE LEVEL: Intermediate—5th and 6th grades

TIME: 45 minutes

NUMBER: Best played with a maximum of 16 students

METHOD OF CHECKING: Media specialist

MATERIALS:
1)   a.   64 3x4" colored posterboard cards bearing a picture of hardware or software, as follows:

> 16 cards with hardware and 16 cards with software; therefore, 32 cards per set, makes 2 sets. Suggested list of hardware and software items are listed in item b, page 222.

> Sample cards appear below. Obtain pictures for cards from old AV catalogs.

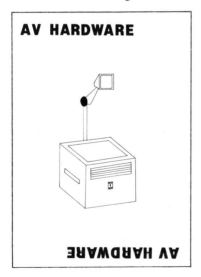

(Materials list continues on page 222)

221

    b.   Lists of:

Hardware	Software
cassette tape recorder	audio cassette
filmstrip projector	filmstrip
16mm projector	16mm film
record player	phonodisc
reel-to-reel tape recorder	reel of audio tape
overhead projector	transparency
opaque projector	book or map
slide projector	slide
Dukane projector	filmstrip and cassette
Dukane projector	filmstrip and phonodisc
film loop projector	8mm film loop
opaque projector	study prints
opaque projector	art prints
TV	video tape
Language Master	audio flashcards
listening station	phonodisc
headset	audio cassette

3)   Large manila envelope (9x12") for the materials.

PROCEDURE:

1)   Four to eight students gather around each set of tables or in a circle on the floor in alphabetical order, according to last name.

2)   Student with the name closest to the beginning of the alphabet is the dealer.

3)   Dealer shuffles cards and places them face down on the table or floor. The cards may be laid out in any pattern, but no two cards should touch each other.

4)   The dealer starts the game by turning face up any two cards, one at a time. All the players look at the two cards as they are turned up, but they are not picked up immediately.

    NOTE: Each player must try to remember the position of each card on the table or floor as they are turned up. There will be more than one possible match for some terms.

5)   If the two cards are a pair, the dealer picks them up, keeps them, and turns up two more cards. The dealer's turn continues as long as the two cards selected are a pair. A pair consists of matching the AV HARDWARE cards to the AV SOFTWARE cards (slide projector to a slide).

6)   If the two cards are not a pair, they are turned face down and left in their original places. This ends the dealer's turn.

7)   After the dealer's turn is over, the player to the left of the dealer continues the game. Play continues around the table or circle on the floor to the left. Cards are only picked up in pairs.

8)   Every time a pair is turned up, the player picks the cards up, keeps them, and continues to try to match cards. The media specialist circulates among the players, verifying pairs, if necessary.

9)   The winner is the player who has accumulated the greatest number of pairs after all of the cards have been matched and picked up.

10) Each player scores one point for each pair gathered during the game.

■ ■ ■

AV RIDDLER

PURPOSE: To gain familiarity with the use of AV hardware.

GRADE LEVEL: Intermediate—5th and 6th grades

TIME: 30 minutes

NUMBER: Best played with a maximum of 16 students

METHOD OF CHECKING: Media specialist

MATERIALS:
1)   14 3x5" index cards with directions for working 14 various pieces of AV equipment. (See "Memory," page 222, for a list of hardware.)

Sample directions for filmstrip projector:

Plug it in.
Turn on the switch.
Insert the filmstrip.
Turn on the lamp.
Focus, using the smallest print.
Advance the filmstrip.

2)   Large manila envelope (10x13") for the materials.

PROCEDURE:
1)   The group is divided into two teams.

2)   The teams form two lines and sit facing the media specialist.

3)   The media specialist draws a card and reads the directions.

4)   The media specialist calls on the first person who raises a hand. If the equipment is identified correctly, a point is scored for that person's team.

5)   If the answer is incorrect, the other team has a chance to score a point by answering correctly.

6)   If neither team answers correctly, the media specialist gives the correct answer and neither team scores a point.

7)   Play continues in this manner until all the cards have been used.

8)   The team with the most points wins.

■ ■ ■

HAVE A HEART

PURPOSE: To gain practice in recalling how to operate AV hardware before the "hands on" experience.

GRADE LEVEL: Intermediate—5th and 6th grades

TIME: 45 minutes

NUMBER: Best played with a maximum of 16 students

METHOD OF CHECKING: Media specialist

MATERIALS:
1) 1 overhead projector.

2) 1 screen.

3) 14 transparencies with pictures of hardware on them; pictures from supply catalogs make good transparencies. (See "Memory," page 222, for a list of hardware.)

4) 14 laminated hearts made of colored posterboard.

5) Large manila envelope (12x15") for the materials.

PROCEDURE:
1) The group is divided into two teams.

2) The teams form two lines and sit facing the screen.

3) The media specialist puts a transparency on the overhead projector.

4) The media specialist calls on the first person who raises a hand to give the oral directions for working the hardware. (See "AV Riddler," page 224, for sample directions.)

5) If correct, the student receives a heart. If the answer is incorrect, the other team gets a chance to get a heart by answering correctly. If neither team can answer fully and correctly, the media specialist gives the complete oral directions and neither team gets a heart.

6) Play continues in this manner.

7) The team with the most hearts wins.

■ ■ ■

$$\diamond$$

LOW BIDDING

$$\diamond$$

PURPOSE: To demonstrate the use of AV hardware.

GRADE LEVEL: Intermediate—5th and 6th grades

TIME: 50 minutes

NUMBER: Best played with a maximum of 16 students

METHOD OF CHECKING: Media specialist

MATERIALS:
1) Appropriate software with AV equipment arranged near plugs.
2) 14 3x4" colored posterboard cards with pictures of equipment on them; pictures from library supply catalogs are suggested. (See "Memory," page 222, for a list of hardware.)
3) 1 die.
4) Large manila envelope (10x13") for the materials.

PROCEDURE:
1) The group is divided into two evenly matched teams.
2) The teams form two lines and sit facing the media specialist.
3) The first two students on each team roll the die to determine who starts the "bidding." Thereafter, the teams alternate starting the bidding.
4) The object is to get the other player to work the hardware for the least amount of points.
5) The media specialist shuffles the cards, draws one card, and holds it up for both teams to see.
6) The team member who starts the bidding may say: "I can work the hardware for 25 points."
7) The second team member may counter: "I can work that hardware for 15 points."

(Procedures continue on page 228)

8) Each player counters with lower point figures until one player says, "Work that hardware!" The object is to reduce the possible number of points for the other team should they be able to work the hardware.

9) The student who must work the hardware finds the equipment and then proceeds to demonstrate how it is to be operated.

10) If the equipment is correctly set up and works, the team scores the number of points bid.

11) If it is incorrectly set up, or if the equipment does not work properly, the media specialist demonstrates the correct procedure and no points are given.

12) The media specialist draws another equipment card and play continues in the same manner, with each team member taking a turn at bidding.

13) The team with the most points wins.

■ ■ ■

APPENDIX I

PROGRESSION OF IMC SKILLS

PARTS OF A BOOK AND IMC VOCABULARY

SAMPLE OBJECTIVE: The elementary student will be able to identify and to tell the uses of various parts of a book (such as author, title, illustrator, title page, table of contents, index, and glossary) as measured by informal, verbal teacher-made tests.

The intermediate grade child will demonstrate with 75 percent accuracy the ability to apply his or her knowledge of the parts of a book and IMC terminology by effective personal use of materials 90 percent of the time, as measured by teacher observation.

Concept	Grade Introduced/Reinforced						
	K	1	2	3	4	5	6
Title, author	X	X	X	X	X	X	X
Call number, illustration, page number		X	X	X	X	X	X
Title page, table of contents, body of book, glossary				X	X	X	X
Copyright date and its meaning				X	X	X	X
Foreword, appendix, index					X	X	X
Bibliography					X	X	X
Dedication, acknowledgments, editor						X	X
Publishing company, place of printing						X	X
List of illustrations, translator						X	X
Author synopsis						X	X
Prologue, epilogue							X
Index of authors, index of titles							X
Index of first lines, index abbreviations							X
Footnotes							X

CARD CATALOG

SAMPLE OBJECTIVE: The elementary grade student, by applying knowledge of the card catalog, will be able to locate information by author, title, and subject 90 percent of the time, as measured by teacher observation.

Concept	Grade Introduced/Reinforced						
	K	1	2	3	4	5	6
Location, definition, purpose, arrangement of trays				X	X	X	X
Identify the three kinds of cards used by distinguishing the different types of entries as they appear on the first line of the catalog card				X	X	X	X
Locate books by author, subject, and title				X	X	X	X
Use of outside and inside guides in the trays				X	X	X	X
Locate the call number on the card, and use this information to find a book on the shelves				X	X	X	X
Type of cards for various kinds of media					X	X	X
Locate the non-print media call number on the card and use this information to find the item in the IMC					X	X	X
Use of cross-references						X	X

SKILLS CHART

LOCATION OF BOOKS AND THE DEWEY DECIMAL CLASSIFICATION SYSTEM

SAMPLE OBJECTIVE: The elementary student will apply knowledge of the arrangement of books in the IMC by being able to independently locate needed items 90 percent of the time, as measured by teacher observation.

Concept	Grade Introduced/Reinforced						
	K	1	2	3	4	5	6
Easy and picture books	X	X	X	X	X	X	X
Meaning of call number on books		X	X	X	X	X	X
Use of call numbers in finding books on shelves			X	X	X	X	X
Fiction and non-fiction location				X	X	X	X
Myths and legends, fairy tales, poetry, science, geography, space, music, sports, history, reference					X	X	X
Individual and collective biography					X	X	X
Ten main divisions of the Dewey Decimal Classification System					X	X	X
Arrangement of books within the Dewey Decimal Classification System						X	X

SPECIAL REFERENCE MATERIALS

SAMPLE OBJECTIVE: The intermediate student will be able to select and use appropriate special reference materials 50 percent of the time with minimal teacher assistance, as measured by teacher observation.

Concept	Grade Introduced/Reinforced						
	K	1	2	3	4	5	6
Atlases, maps, and globes			X	X	X	X	X
Special references:							
almanacs					X	X	X
biographical dictionaries						X	X
Junior Book of Authors, More Junior Authors, and *Children's Literature Review*						X	X
Vertical files:							
pictures and pamphlet materials, periodical articles, newspaper clippings						X	X
Selection of appropriate reference tool						X	X
Special indexes:							
National Geographic Index, 1947-1976; Abridged Reader's Guide to Periodical Literature; Poetry Index; Short Story Index; Plays Index							X
Effective use of reference tools							X

DICTIONARY REFERENCE SKILLS

SAMPLE OBJECTIVE: The intermediate student, given the need to define or spell a word, will be able to apply a knowledge of dictionary skills to locate the needed word 90 percent of the time, as measured by teacher observation.

Concept	Grade Introduced/Reinforced						
	K	1	2	3	4	5	6
Alphabetical arrangement of the dictionary		X	X	X	X	X	X
Division of dictionary into front, middle, back parts				X	X	X	X
Locate words in the dictionary by using guide words				X	X	X	X
Selective use of various meanings for words					X	X	X
Antonyms, homonyms, synonyms, syllabication, thumb index						X	X
Unabridged and special dictionaries						X	X
Locate material in special dictionaries						X	X
Find abbreviations and parts of speech						X	X
Locate hyphenated words, special information, word history, prefixes, suffixes, pictures, and illustrations						X	X

ENCYCLOPEDIA REFERENCE SKILLS

SAMPLE OBJECTIVE: The intermediate student will be able to show the ability to use an encyclopedia by successfully locating information 80 percent of the time without teacher assistance, as measured by teacher observation.

Concept	Grade Introduced/Reinforced						
	K	1	2	3	4	5	6
Location and purpose of encyclopedias in the library				X	X	X	X
Arrangement and types of information found in encyclopedias				X		X	X
Difference between encyclopedia and dictionary				X	X	X	X
Use of the index in an encyclopedia					X	X	X
Ability to obtain information from encyclopedias					X	X	X
Use of cross-reference and related subject references						X	X
Organize facts for specific purposes through the use of the encyclopedia							X

NON-PRINT MEDIA REFERENCE SKILLS

SAMPLE OBJECTIVE: The intermediate grade student will be able to show the ability to use non-print media for reference by successfully locating information 75 percent of the time without teacher assistance, as measured by teacher observation.

Concept	Grade Introduced/Reinforced						
	K	1	2	3	4	5	6
Ability to obtain information from non-print media					X	X	X
Organize facts for specific purposes through the use of non-print media						X	X

USE OF EQUIPMENT

SAMPLE OBJECTIVE: The elementary student will be able to demonstrate proficiency in using equipment 95 percent of the time without teacher assistance, as measured by teacher observation.

Concept	Grade Introduced/Reinforced						
	K	1	2	3	4	5	6
Language Master, headset	X	X	X	X	X	X	X
Cassette recorder, record player, filmstrip viewer, listening center		X	X	X	X	X	X
Overhead projector				X	X	X	X
Filmstrip projector, Dukane projector, film loop projector, opaque projector					X	X	X
16mm projector, slide projector						X	X
Reel-to-reel tape recorder, video tape recorder							X

APPENDIX II

REFERENCE BOOKS AND DESCRIPTIONS
USED IN THE GAMES

REFERENCE BOOKS AND DESCRIPTIONS
USED IN THE GAMES

Bartlett, John. *Bartlett's Familiar Quotations.* Boston: Little, c1968.

Gives the source of each quotation listed.

Brewton, John. *Index to Children's Poetry.* New York: H. W. Wilson, c1973.

A dictionary index of 130 collections of poems for children and youth—with title, author, subject, and first line entries.

Children's Literature Review, Vol. I, II, and III. Detroit, MI: Gale Research Co., c1976.

Arranged in alphabetical order by the author's last name, giving an excerpt of recent reviews of both fiction and non-fiction for children and young people.

Commire, Anne. *Something about the Author.* Detroit, MI: Gale Research Co., c1971.

Facts and pictures about contemporary authors and illustrators of books for young people.

Commire, Anne. *Yesterday's Authors of Books for Children.* Detroit, MI: Gale Research Co., c1977.

Facts and pictures about authors and illustrators of books for young people from early times to 1960.

Couzens, Reginald. *The Stories of the Months and Days.* Detroit, MI: Gale Research Co., c1971.

Provides the myths and legends behind the names of the months and days of the week. The attributes, feats, and significance of the gods and heroes whose names adorn the calendar are explained also.

Evans, Ivor. *Brewer's Dictionary of Phrase and Fable.* New York: Harper and Row, c1970.

An extensive alphabetical list of classical references. Contains some slang phrases and expressions that arose from World War II.

Funk, Wilfred. *Word Origins and Their Romantic Stories.* New York: Funk and Wagnalls, c1950.

Shows the life history of a word, which makes its present meaning clearer. Arranged in chapters dealing with certain areas such as house, garden, politics, and so on.

Greet, W. Cabell. *In Other Words: A Junior Thesaurus.* Glenview, IL: Scott, Foresman, c1969.

An alphabetical listing of words with synonyms and their meanings.

Halliburton, Richard. *Book of Marvels.* New York: Bobbs-Merrill, c1941.

This book is filled with pictures of the world's cities, mountains, temples, and maps to show where they are located. The information is related in story-book style.

Hone, William. *The Every-Day Book.* Detroit, MI: Gale Research Co., c1967.

For every day of the year there are articles, poems, historical notes, essays on folklore and customs, religious information, and illustrations.

Kane, Joseph. *Famous First Facts.* New York: H. W. Wilson Co., c1973.

An alphabetical listing of the first time that something happened.

Kingman, Lee. *Newbery & Caldecott Medal Books, 1966-1975.* Boston: Horn Book Inc., c1975.

For each year there is an excerpt from the book, a short summary of the work, and the acceptance speech by the author.

Kravitz, David. *Who's Who in Greek and Roman Mythology.* New York: Crown Publishers, c1976.

An alphabetical listing of mythological characters with entries that emphasize and clarify intrafamily relationships.

Kunitz, Stanley. *Junior Book of Authors.* New York: H. W. Wilson Co., c1951.

Biographical and autobiographical sketches of authors and illustrators of books for children and young people.

McWhirter, Norris. *Guinness Book of World Records.* New York: Bantam Books, c1977.

Claims to include the greatest human achievements of the century. The book uses a table of contents and an index to arrange the material.

Melbo, Irving. *Our Country's National Parks,* Vol. I and II. New York: Bobbs-Merrill, c1973.

A story of all national parks presenting historical, factual, and scientific information.

Montreville, Doris de. *Third Book of Junior Authors.* New York: H. W. Wilson Co., c1972.

Sketches of authors are in alphabetical order by the form of author's name appearing most frequently on the title page.

Morris, Richard B., ed. *Encyclopedia of American History.* New York: Harper and Row, c1976.

One volume of essential historical facts in both chronological and topical order. Dates, events, achievements, and persons of importance are given in narrative form.

National Geographic Index, 1947-1976. Washington: National Geographic Society, c1977.

An alphabetical listing of more than 14,000 entries spanning 30 years, this helps find information on different articles.

Palmer, Robin. *A Dictionary of Mythical Places.* New York: Walch, c1975.

An alphabetically arranged dictionary of mythical, legendary, and famous places briefly describing the origin, location, and major characteristics of each place.

Roget, Peter M. *Roget's Thesaurus of English Words and Phrases.* New York: St. Martin's Press, c1965.

An alphabetical listing of words with synonyms.

Ross, Frank. *Stories of the States.* New York: Crowell, c1969.

An alphabetical listing of the fifty states and the United States territories, giving major characteristics of each and a short history.

Shaw, John M. *Childhood in Poetry.* Detroit, MI: Gale Research Co., c1967-1976.

A catalog with biographical and critical annotations of the books of English and American poets comprising the Shaw Childhood in Poetry Collection in the library of Florida State University.

Worrelle, Estelle. *Early American Costume.* Harrisburg, PA: Stackpole Books, c1975.

Each chapter gives a description of the period's costumes and a picture, starting in 1580 and ending in 1850.

Worth, Fred L. *The Trivia Encyclopedia.* Los Angeles: Brooke House, c1974.

An alphabetical listing of interesting and trivial facts that are difficult to find elsewhere.

DATE DUE

DEMCO 38-297

DATE DUE

DEMCO 38-297